PRAISE FOR
RELEASE YOUR INNER DRIVE

Seductively readable and yet also impressively evidence-based, this beautifully produced book represents an exceptional distillation of research around motivation. It's a tough art to keep the message simple without straying into the simplistic badlands, or risk patronising a hyper-vigilant teenaged audience, and the authors carry this off remarkably well. Time-starved teachers will find much classroom-ready material to use here too.

Dr Barry Hymer, Emeritus Professor of Psychology
in Education, University of Cumbria

Bradley Busch and Edward Watson have sifted through a wealth of insight from cognitive and behavioural psychology into our strengths and weaknesses as students – and humans – and transformed it into a helpful, usable guide. Attractive summaries are helpfully combined with clear explanations of the underlying ideas. Applying just a handful of the ideas would, I suspect, help anyone to both study better and flourish while doing so.

Harry Fletcher-Wood, Associate Dean, Institute for Teaching

I would recommend this wonderful book, aimed at a teen audience, as both a parent and a teacher. It is packed with evidence-based (thoroughly referenced), practical tips to support our youngsters; for example, to help them make their learning more memorable or to help them live less stressful lives. The very clear graphics are a real strength of the book and allow the reader to dip in and out. I couldn't help but proffer its pages to my son, now preparing for his next set of exams. Very teen-friendly!

Hélène Galdin O'Shea, teacher and researchEd organiser

If anyone is looking to develop a growth mindset and generally tackle life in a more positive and confident way then this book is a must-read. Complex concepts are presented in a simple manner in order for the reader to take away key messages and apply them across a number of relevant situations. The authors must be commended on providing a unique format, allowing readers to retain important information, which underpins the effective thinking and behaviour needed in order to thrive.

Ian Mitchell, Performance Psychologist,
Wales' national senior football team

D1329276

Bradley and Edward have written an accessible, comprehensive guide to implementing the latest research into motivation, self-control and neuroscience to help you to get better at ... well, everything! Their book breaks down the process of goal-setting, self-discipline, coping with challenge, learning and achievement into a series of tips and tricks, rendered into easy-to-understand lists which make great resources for students, teachers or anyone trying to do that little bit better. All the key information for each topic is captured in an eye-catching single page, meaning that the book serves as a catalogue of self-help guides. But these single pages are supported by helpful detail, explaining how and why you should follow the advice. Each of the guides is sourced with detailed research from the fields of psychology, health and neuroscience, giving the reader confidence that these easily digestible chunks are much more than just platitudes or motivational slogans. *Release Your Inner Drive* will be a great resource for anyone involved in education and learning – or, indeed, anyone who "wants to get good at stuff".

Chris Hildrew, Head Teacher, Churchill Academy and Sixth Form

I worked with Bradley during the most stressful time of my life, competing in a Paralympic Games. By using a lot of the techniques in this book I have become a more successful person, not only in my career but also outside of it. I have changed the way I view failure and this is what has helped me the most. The techniques are simple but they have had a massive impact, it's almost hard to believe. This book teaches us how to get big rewards from simply changing the way we view and handle what life throws at us. For any-one looking to better themselves in some way, no matter how big or small, this is the book for you.

Jordanne Whiley, MBE, winner of nine grand slam
tennis tournaments and Paralympic medallist

This is a really helpful resource for students, parents and teachers who want to get a handle on the most effective ways of revising, goal-setting and handling stress. A great balance of clear infographics and research on peak performance across a range of disciplines – aspirational and reassuring in equal measure.

Mary Myatt, education adviser, speaker
and author of *Hopeful Schools*

Really enjoyed the book – there are some real strengths to the design along-side the wealth of tips and knowledge. I love the infographics, which offer a quick and easy way of getting the key information across.

Chris Thurston, Head of Education and Welfare, Watford Football Club

Release Your Inner Drive by Bradley Busch and Edward Watson suggests strategies to help young people develop productive habits and offers practical tips for setting goals and taking control of where they are going and how they intend to get there.

Based on the principle of growth mindset the book is clearly structured and easy to read, with eye-catching and light-hearted graphics, designed to appeal to its target audience, but also with something to offer to teachers and parents who support and encourage young people.

The book prompts reflection and recommends actively seeking out and acting on feedback in order to boost confidence and enhance achievements. It emphasises the importance of resisting perfectionism and looking after ourselves by finding a healthy balance in our lives, including specific advice for controlling our use of mobile devices and social media.

Useful quotations, inspirational stories and specific examples, including references to recent research, strengthen the advice offered as to how students can ensure revision is effective and examination performance is positive. The book ends with a call to action and a very useful, extensive list of references to prompt further reading.

Jill Berry, leadership consultant and author of *Making the Leap*

Release Your Inner Drive is an excellent guide to understanding how to improve. The authors distil a huge volume of peer-reviewed research on performance psychology and neuroscience into a number of key areas and provide simple and effective strategies to develop in each one. The book works especially well as a quick reference guide. This is a resource to keep returning to for some gentle reminders of how to regain control during times of stress. Key questions are provided throughout that can be applied in education, sport and general life. It's a book perfect for parents and teachers who want to enable children and young adults to develop the mental skills required for a positive mindset.

Nick Cooper, Director, Performance Solutions

Release Your Inner Drive is a fantastically useful book, providing practical advice for students. Written in straightforward language and full of helpful graphics, it explains in tangible steps how to develop the attitudes, mindsets and habits that are crucial to success at school and in life, such as confidence, well-being, resilience, learning from mistakes and improving memory. Crucially, this advice is evidence-based and has been distilled from high-quality research in cognitive psychology and neuroscience. I have never come across a clearer explanation for students of how to handle the complexities of motivation, mindset and performance.

Jonnie Noakes, Head of Teaching and Learning, Eton College

Release Your Inner Drive very skilfully applies well-grounded, contemporary psychological concepts to an array of achievement situations. The infographics communicate complex theory in a really digestible way, designed to help readers make sense of the mental aspects of performance, and apply thinking skills within their particular domain. As an academic and practitioner, I think the inclusion of research and references is really important and I particularly appreciated this aspect of the book. Many of the graphics are eye-catching, but also accurate, helping people to remember what they read, which helps them apply what they read to their world. The graphical way in which the content is presented allows the reader to easily understand the tools being introduced, and the theory behind the tools. Information is chunked in such a way that the reader is able to take away key pieces of information easily. The advice is not only useful for people wishing to fulfil their potential, it is also important for well-being. Indeed, many of the concepts are as much about maintaining and enhancing well-being as they are about achievement. My favourite part was Chapter 10, where growth mindset is really clearly applied. I also like the fact that the reader is given options as to how to use the book, prior to and after reading it.

I would recommend this book to anyone who is interested in fulfilling their potential or inquisitive about how they can harness psychology to improve their performance.

Dr Martin J. Turner, Lecturer in Sport and
Exercise Psychology, Staffordshire University

RELEASE YOUR INNER DRIVE

EVERYTHING YOU NEED TO KNOW ABOUT
HOW TO GET GOOD AT STUFF

Bradley Busch and Edward Watson

Crown House Publishing Limited
www.crownhouse.co.uk

First published by

Crown House Publishing Ltd
Crown Buildings, Bancyfelin, Carmarthen, Wales, SA33 5ND, UK
www.crownhouse.co.uk

and

Crown House Publishing Company LLC
PO Box 2223, Williston, VT 05495
www.crownhousepublishing.com

British Library Cataloguing-in-Publication Data
A catalogue entry for this book is available from the British Library.

Print ISBN 978-178583199-7
Mobi ISBN 978-178583239-0
ePub ISBN 978-178583240-6
ePDF ISBN 978-178583241-3

LCCN 2017939649

Printed and bound in the UK by
Gomer Press, Llandysul, Ceredigion

ACKNOWLEDGEMENTS

Firstly, thank you to our publisher, David, for having faith in our work, our copy-editor, Emma, for correcting our million and one typpos and grammar errors and to all those at Crown House Publishing who have helped us along the way. Thank you also to our exceptional graphics designer, Luis A. Miguel, for creating such brilliant pieces of art which form the backbone of this book.

Thank you to the thousands of teachers, parents, students and athletes that we have had the honour and pleasure of working with. Thank you for helping to shape our philosophies and ideas on how to help people release their inner drive.

Thanks also to the many researchers who have clocked up so many hours investigating and studying how people get good at stuff – we hope we did your research justice.

Thanks to all the people who have been an integral part of the InnerDrive team over the years, but in particular DC, Blythe, Marayka, Claire, Harry, Isobel, Izzy, Emily, Tom, Hannah, Ollie, Fudge and Twiggy. We have loved working with you all and you have blessed us with your humour and your hard work. And a special thank you to Dan without whom we would never have met and shared such good times together.

Lastly, and of course most importantly, a huge thank you to our wives, Pippa and Helen, for putting up with us. You have made us better people and continuously inspire us. To the rest of our families, whose love and support has helped us in so many ways over so many years, thank you.

Dear Tirion

Your Mum

Says Do this

and Release your Inner Drive

Edward + Bradley

CONTENTS

HOW TO READ
THIS BOOK

9 Ways to Read This Book

1

Find a graphic you like

2

From front to back

3

From back to front

4

Choose a topic you like

5

Only look at the pictures

6

Pick a random page

7

Jump around

8

Ask a friend to pick a page at random

9

On the loo

RELEASE YOUR INNER DRIVE

Have you ever wondered how people get really good at stuff? It turns out that whatever area you look at, there are a collection of habits that help people to get good at what they do. The strategies that create these habits can be learnt and used by anyone, and that is what this book is about.

HERE'S THE DEAL

Let's face it: sometimes reading a book can be a bit of a struggle. This book is *not* that book. Your life is way too interesting and important to let that happen. This book is filled with tips that have been proven to help people release their inner drive.

As well as that, it's got loads of pictures in it. Each subject stands alone, so you don't have to read the book in any particular order. If you just look at the graphics and take some action as a result, it will help. If you want to dig a bit deeper, then we have written some words after most of the pictures to give a bit more of an explanation.

Feel free to get in contact with us and let us know what you think. You can do this via Twitter @Inner_Drive, through our website www.innerdrive.co.uk or by emailing us at info@innerdrive.co.uk.

We would love to hear from you.

Here is our first graphic with some ideas on how you might read this book. Enjoy.

CHAPTER 1

DECIDE WHERE YOU ARE GOING

OWN THE DESTINATION

11 Ways to Improve Your Goal Setting

Have a Long Term Goal
Gives your motivation a boost.

Have a Short Term Goal
Helps you maintain focus.

Make it Challenging but Realistic
Aim high so that you really push yourself.

What's the Why?
Give a reason why your goal is important.

Make it Specific
Specific not vague terms make it
easier to monitor progress.

Focus on Skills
Focus on developing your skills,
not just on the end outcome.

Be Flexible
If the situation changes,
tweak your goals.

Share Your Goals
If other people know about them,
they may be able to help you.

Ensure There is Trust
People work harder on achieving a goal if they
trust the person who has set them that goal.

Consider Potential Obstacles
This allows you to come up with a plan,
ensuring that you are fully prepared.

Monitor Progress
This helps you stay on the right track
and to adjust as needed.

BE THE MASTER OF YOUR FATE

During his 27 years in prison, Nelson Mandela used to reflect on a poem to help him get through the difficult days and maintain his motivation to bring democracy and freedom to South Africa. That poem was 'Invictus' by William Ernest Henley.[1]

Invictus

Out of the night that covers me,
Black as the pit from pole to pole,
I thank whatever gods may be
For my unconquerable soul.

In the fell clutch of circumstance
I have not winced nor cried aloud.
Under the bludgeoning of chance
My head is bloody, but unbowed.

Beyond this place of wrath and tears
Looms but the Horror of the shade,
And yet the menace of the years
Finds, and shall find me, unafraid.

It matters not how strait the gate,
How charged with punishments the scroll,
I am the master of my fate,
I am the captain of my soul.

HOW TO DO GOAL SETTING RIGHT

'Invictus' is about realising that you do have some control over your destiny. We don't always know what is going to happen to us, but we can decide which direction we point in and how we react to the unexpected. Being the master of your fate and captain of your soul means actively choosing what to do with your life and how to live it.

Long term vision and short term focus

Focusing on a long term vision helps you overcome the setbacks that happen along the way.[2] They provide light at the end of the tunnel, especially on the dark days when you struggle. Setting short term goals (i.e. what you need to do this week) helps as well. Breaking down a seemingly impossible and distant dream into simple, tangible steps makes the goal much more achievable. These small steps can help to keep you on the right path, and clocking up regular wins along the way provides a boost to motivation and confidence.

Challenging but realistic

There is a well-known phrase, "a man's reach should exceed his grasp". It is important to stretch yourself and not to settle for what you have already achieved. If you settle for what you can easily achieve, it is harder to grow and improve.[3] Constantly setting challenging goals will boost your motivation to work harder and give you a higher sense of accomplishment once the goal has been reached.

What's your why?

Martin Luther King Jr knew the power of having a clear sense of purpose. He once said, "If it falls your lot to be a street sweeper, sweep streets like Michelangelo painted pictures, sweep streets like Beethoven composed music ... Sweep streets like Shakespeare wrote poetry." Sweeping like Shakespeare means knowing what you are doing, knowing why you are doing it and doing it to the very best of your ability. Having this sense of purpose and clarity helps to boost your determination and resilience.

Make it specific and focus on skills

Try to avoid vague terms when setting your goals as this makes it harder to monitor progress. Aiming to improve is a good thing. Identifying which areas you want to improve is better. Set goals that focus on improving your skills and not just on what you want to achieve.[4] Most of the time the final outcome relies on being able to execute your skills under pressure, so make that what you focus on.

Consider potential obstacles

This may sound a bit negative at first. Why would you want to consider what is standing in the way of you and your goals? Wouldn't it be better to be 100% positive and confident? It turns out that only thinking about the positives can do more harm than good, as it can lead to over-confidence, daydreaming and procrastination, and leaves you ill-prepared for potential setbacks.[5] If you anticipate what obstacles you may face, you can effectively prepare and plan for them.

Monitor your progress and be flexible

You can't always predict how a situation may turn out. Life has a funny habit of throwing up random events. If the situation changes, your goals may need to be tweaked.[6] Monitoring, tweaking and amending your goals is the hallmark of a mature learner. It helps to maintain your motivation over long periods of time.

CHAPTER 2

MASTER YOURSELF

IT BEGINS WITH YOU

5 Questions to Help Develop a Growth Mindset

1. Do you spend more time arguing or actioning the feedback you get?

2. Is the effort today worth the reward tomorrow?

3. Do you want honest feedback or do you want me to make you feel good?

4. Do you feel threatened by successful people or do you want to learn how they did it?

5. You've had a setback. What would you do differently next time?

QUESTIONS THAT ENCOURAGE A GROWTH MINDSET

Do you believe that your abilities are set in stone and probably decided at birth, or do you think that you have the capability to grow and improve? It turns out that how you answer this question has big implications for how fast you learn.

Those who believe that their abilities are set in stone have a 'fixed mindset' and those who believe that you can develop have a 'growth mindset'.[7] Having a growth mindset means knowing that smart is not something you are, but something you get.[8]

People with a growth mindset:

■ Seek out better feedback.

■ Want to persist at difficult tasks for longer.

■ Cope better with change.

■ Have lower levels of stress.

■ Have better self-control.[9]

So how does one go about developing a growth mindset? Consider how you would answer these questions.

Do you spend more time arguing or actioning the feedback you get?

Some people spend more time arguing against the feedback they are given than actually using it. People who argue with the feedback they receive are often worried that they are being judged. They would rather drown in compliments than be saved by criticism.

Asking for and using feedback is one of the simplest ways to get better at a task. If someone is willing to offer you their time and effort to give you feedback, then cherish it. Ultimately, those who learn from the feedback they are given improve the fastest.

Is the effort today worth the reward tomorrow?

Having a growth mindset means you are happy to work and sacrifice now in order to get the rewards later on. Those with a fixed mindset often want an easy and simple life. This is fine if that is your choice, but it is important to know that in the long run it is not likely to lead to you fulfilling your potential. Think back to your proudest achievement – chances are that you had to work really hard beforehand in order to achieve it.

Do you feel threatened by successful people or do you want to find out how they did it?

Constantly comparing yourself with others can have a negative impact on your confidence, motivation, self-management and academic performance.[10] Instead of feeling threatened by other people's success, a more healthy approach is to want to learn from them. How do they do what they do? What is their mindset like? How have they overcome setbacks? Once you have the mindset that you can get better, you start to see other people's success as an opportunity to learn and improve.

You've had a setback. What would you do differently next time?

This question can help to stop you from dwelling on the past and allow you to refocus on making the future better. Psychologists use the term 'metacognition' to describe being aware and in control of your own thought processes. Asking what you would do differently is a great example of this: it helps you to analyse thoughts and tweak them. Developing metacognitive skills has been linked to better grades in school[11] and higher levels of resilience.[12]

Do you want honest feedback or do you want me to make you feel good?

Some people would rather drown in praise than be saved by criticism. Getting good honest feedback (and using it) is one of the quickest ways to get better.

5 WAYS TO DEVELOP A GROWTH MINDSET

1 **Don't Rush to "I Can't"** When people start a new task, or are doing one that is very difficult, it is sometimes tempting to say "I can't do this" or "I can't be bothered". With a bit of effort, you might surprise yourself by how well you can do the task and how much you enjoy it.

2 **The Power of "Yet"** This simple word can have a big impact. There is a huge difference between saying "I am not good at this" and "I am not good at this yet". By adding the word "yet", it suggests you may get there with some hard work and resilience.

3 **Ask Yourself** "What would I do differently next time?" This is a great question to ask after a setback. It stops you dwelling on the past and helps you reflect and focus on what you need to improve on in the future.

4 **Failing Better** Everyone experiences failure at some stage in their life. But can you fail better? This doesn't mean failing more often. One way to fail better is if you ask someone for feedback and then use it.

5 **Try New Things** Having a sense of curiosity and courage can be really helpful. It can help you learn new things. Sometimes new equals the unknown which equals scary. But it doesn't have to be this way. Sometimes new experiences can be the most rewarding and most exciting.

IMPROVING SELF-CONTROL

If you were offered a marshmallow and told that if you waited for a while you would get two marshmallows, would you be able to wait or would you eat the first marshmallow straight away? In the early 1970s, researcher Walter Mischel offered young children this very choice, and the results changed forever how we view self-control.[13]

Mischel tracked the participants in his study and found that, ten years later, the children who were able to wait and not eat the marshmallow immediately were rated as being more attentive, verbally fluent, and academically and socially competent, and were better able to deal with frustration and stress.[14]

It seems that the ability to resist a reward now in order to gain better long term rewards is a vital life skill. Here are some tips to help you resist your marshmallows.

5 Ways to Improve Self-Control

1 Remove the Temptation
People who focus on the temptation are more likely to engage in it. So make sure your environment helps you perform to your best.

2 Maintain Good Energy Levels
Self-control requires energy. Don't underestimate the power of a good night's sleep and a healthy diet.

3 Set Specific Goals
Focusing on what you want to achieve helps you persist with your goal and helps you prioritise your actions.

4 Use Negative Associations
Associate something bad with what's distracting you and you'll be less likely to do it.

5 Develop a Plan
Generate a plan for how to behave in a specific situation. This will boost your self-control.

Remove the temptation

People who focus on the temptation are more likely to engage in it. Results from the original marshmallow study found that people were more likely to eat the marshmallow if it was in sight. If you know what tempts you, remove it from your environment before it distracts you.

Maintain good energy levels

It is much harder to control yourself if you are feeling tired and drained. Self-control requires energy.[15] This is one of the reasons why getting a regular good night's sleep, having a healthy balanced diet and eating a good breakfast is so important.

Focus on what you want

By reminding yourself of your goals and why you want to achieve them, you are more likely to be able to keep temptations and distractions at bay.[16] Next time you catch yourself being distracted, remind yourself what matters to you.

Use negative associations

If you can associate the behaviour that is distracting you with something bad, then you are less likely to do it.[17] A good starting point here is to have a frank conversation with yourself about why the tempting behaviour is unhelpful and how it can hurt your chances of achieving your goal.

Develop a plan

Generating a plan for how you want to behave in a specific situation will boost your self-control. This can take the form of "If X happens, I will do Y". This is a particularly effective strategy during stressful situations which require you to think carefully and quickly.

7 Ways to Overcome Procrastination

1 Do the Task for Just a Few Minutes
Use the Zeigarnik effect – once you start something your brain remains alert until you finish it.

2 Do the Hard Tasks First
Doing the hard tasks whilst your brain is still fresh means you are less likely to give up on them or procrastinate.

3 Believe in Your Ability
You can do it, just implement the skills and strategies you have learnt to self-regulate.

4 Manage Your Environment
Control it, don't let it control you. Get rid of distractions, especially that lovely beguiling phone of yours.

5 Set Yourself Short Deadlines
Impending deadlines get you going. So go ahead and set yourself short deadlines.

6 Model Success
Who do you know that has done this task well? What did they do? Copy what they did.

7 Make the Task Harder
Sounds counterintuitive but it can make the task more interesting.

OVERCOMING PROCRASTINATION

Procrastination is nothing new. More than 100 years ago, psychologist William James wrote that "nothing is so fatiguing as the eternal hanging on of an uncompleted task". You are not the only one who does it either: 75% of people consider themselves procrastinators, with 50% doing it to a level that they think is problematic.[18]

Overcoming procrastination is just another success skill that can be learnt through practice, effort and self-discipline. There is an old Chinese proverb that says, "The best time to plant a tree was 20 years ago. The second best time is now." Or, to put it another way, do not put off until tomorrow what you can achieve today.

So here are some tips to help you procrastinate a little less.

Do the task for just a few minutes

Not only do procrastinators spend longer distracting themselves doing the 'wrong things', but they also delay starting the 'right things'.[19] To combat this, use the Zeigarnik effect to your advantage.[20] The Zeigarnik effect describes the observation that once you start a task, your brain remains alert until you finish it. Starting a task is often the hardest part. If you can start it for just a few minutes, the brain's desire to see it through to completion will then take over.

Do the hard tasks first

Our biological clock, known as our circadian rhythm, ensures that we are often at our most alert at around 10 a.m., after which we suffer a mid-afternoon dip. The harder the tasks are, the more energy and concentration you will need to complete them. It makes sense to do the hardest and most important tasks early because trying to start them when you are tired is difficult and will often result in you putting them off for another day.

Believe in your ability

Those who believe they won't be successful at a task are more likely to procrastinate.[21] Start small and build up. As you clock up more successes your confidence will increase, as will your motivation to keep going.

Set yourself short deadlines

The further away an event is, the more likely you are to procrastinate.[22] We often think that we have more time than we do. This is called the 'planning fallacy'. You can overcome this by breaking down the task into short sections and setting yourself a deadline for each part. This will stop you from putting it off and keep you on track.

Make the task harder

This may sound counterintuitive. Surely, a harder task will make you want to put off the task even more? Apparently not. People tend to report a higher sense of satisfaction if they have successfully completed a difficult task.[23] In the United States they ask, "Is the juice worth the squeeze?" Making fresh orange juice requires hard work to squeeze the fruit. But often the harder the squeeze, the tastier the juice.

7 Tips to Help You Concentrate Better

Eat Breakfast ①
Students who eat breakfast score better on attention and memory tests. Cereals that are rich in complex carbohydrates are good as they fuel your brain.

Exercise at ② Lunchtime
A study by researchers at Bristol University found that a 45-minute workout at lunchtime significantly improved people's concentration, mood and ability to do their job.

Worry About it ③ a Little More
In certain situations, a bit of stress may make you perform better. The extra worry releases adrenaline which increases the intensity of your focus.

④ Don't Think Don't
Attempts at thought suppression make you think about the thing you want to avoid more and distract you from the task at hand.

⑤ Drink Some Water
If you are just 1% dehydrated your concentration drops dramatically. Students who take water into an exam have been found to outperform their thirsty peers.

⑥ The Great Outdoors
Those who take a walk in green space return feeling more focused than those who have a break walking in urban areas.

⑦ Pictures of Nature
No green space near you? No problem. Studies have found that those who look at photos of nature, especially those with water in them, feel the same sort of benefits.

9 Ways to Overcome FOMO

Fear Of Missing Out

1 You Can't Do It All
You can't be in two places at once.

2 Be Where Your Feet Are
Focus on the present moment.

3 Choose Experiences Over Status Updates
Do things that matter to you, not just what you can write about online.

4 Do One Thing at a Time
It's hard to multi-task, so focus on one thing at a time.

5 Minimise Distractions
Sometimes it's good to turn your phone off.

6 Ask WIN Questions
What's Important Now?

7 The Grass Isn't Always Greener
People often seem happier on Facebook than they actually are.

8 Limit Time on Social Media
Excessive use of social media is linked to FOMO.

9 Enjoy the Journey
Embrace the process, as well as the outcome.

OVERCOMING FOMO

FOMO stands for the Fear Of Missing Out. It happens when people worry that they will miss out on something great. It is the fear that you won't be part of something that everyone else will be talking about. FOMO has some negative consequences. Trying to do everything often results in you doing very little of anything. It also increases your stress and anxiety. So how can you overcome FOMO?

You can't do it all

You can't be in two places at once. This is what is known as an 'opportunity cost'. For each task you take on there is something else that you cannot do. There is a cost for each opportunity you choose. Understanding this will help to reduce your FOMO.

Be where your feet are

Focus on the present moment. We spend so much time focusing on the past or worrying about the future. Being where your feet are is about focusing on the here and now. Although it is good to learn from the past and be motivated by the future, it is important to have a strong focus on the present.

Choose experiences over status updates

Do things that matter to you, not just what you can write about online. People often give an overly positive and unrealistic representation of their lives on social media. Don't try to compete with these shadows – it is impossible to catch them. If you are experiencing an event and already planning to make it your Facebook status, then there is a chance you are missing out on the moment. Taking yourself offline every now and again is also a healthy strategy, as spending too much time on social media is a sure sign of FOMO.[25]

Do one thing at a time

It is really hard to multi-task. To show how difficult it is, try counting down from 100 in nines whilst also writing out the alphabet backwards. For things that take conscious effort, it is almost impossible to do two things at once. Multi-tasking is a bit of a myth. Those people who appear to do it are actually very good at switching between tasks rapidly. But this switching takes up valuable time and mental energy. If accuracy is important, it is better to fully focus on one thing, finish it and then do another.

Ask WIN questions

A WIN question is when you ask yourself, "What's Important Now?" This is a good way to help you prioritise. If you can't do everything at once, it's better to start on the things that are most important to you.

Enjoy the journey

Embrace the process as well as the outcome. Outcomes can sometimes be anti-climactic. However, working hard and dedicating yourself to your goals rarely is. Life is short and time is precious. If you only focus on the end product, and not the process that got you there, you may miss opportunities to learn, improve and enjoy yourself along the way.

MANAGING THAT PHONE

Many years ago, the Greek philosopher Socrates worried that there was a trend sweeping the nation that would "produce forgetfulness in the minds of those who learn to use it, because they will not practise their memory". The trend he was talking about was writing things down. Today, many people worry that mobile phones will have the same impact.[26]

Mobile phones allow us to communicate in a way that would have seemed impossible just a generation ago. We now have access to all the information we could want at our fingertips, we can listen to almost any song ever made and watch any movie.

As with most great advances in technology, it is how we use it that matters. A recent survey found that 81% of people never turn their phone off, even when in bed.[27] The next two graphics give a brief overview of some of the downsides to using your phone too much and also some strategies to manage it better.

6 Reasons
to Put Your Phone Away

Lowers Concentration

Having your phone out while doing homework or revision has been shown to reduce performance by 20%.

Increases FOMO

Fear of Missing Out (FOMO), or the compulsive need to know what others are doing, leads to worse moods and increased anxiety.

Increases Stress and Anxiety

Overuse of mobile phones leads to increased anxiety, feelings of loneliness and low self-esteem. Reliance on mobile phones can cause irritation, frustration and impatience.

Warps Your View of Reality

Nobody is as happy as they seem on Facebook or as wise as they appear on Twitter.

Reduces Memory

Instant messages are distracting, which often leads to forgetfulness.

Makes You Sleep Worse

Prolonged use of a mobile phone leads to poor sleep quality and duration. The backlight on your phone delays the release of melatonin, which is a hormone important for sleep.

12 Ways to Manage Your Mobile Phone

1 SET YOURSELF A TIME LIMIT

2 TURN IT OFF

3 LIMIT NOTIFICATIONS IN SETTINGS

4 DON'T HAVE IT OUT NEXT TO YOU WHILST YOU REVISE

5 LET FRIENDS KNOW WHEN YOU WILL BE BACK ONLINE

6 TURN DOWN THE BACKLIGHT OF YOUR PHONE NEAR BEDTIME

7 USE GOING ON YOUR PHONE AS A REWARD

8 RESIST THE URGE TO REPLY TO EVERY MESSAGE

9 GIVE IT TO YOUR MUM OR DAD TO LOOK AFTER
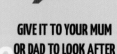

10 TURN IT ON TO AIRPLANE MODE

11 DON'T HAVE IT IN YOUR ROOM WHEN YOU SLEEP

12 TURN YOUR PHONE ON 'SILENT'

CHAPTER 3

FAIL BETTER

THE POWER OF FAILURE

6 Ways That Setbacks Can Help

Use your failure to ...

 Increase your motivation to succeed

 Learn more about what you need to do better or differently

 Develop your compassion and empathy

 Increase your resilience and determination

 Prompt you to ask for help

 Make your final accomplishment more rewarding

HOW FAILURE CAN HELP YOU

It may seem strange for a book about how to get good at stuff to have a chapter about failure. From a young age, most of us learn that

failure = bad = avoid at all costs.

But setbacks and disappointments along the journey are inevitable. We all slip up and make mistakes. What matters is how you react to them.

Failure is not fatal – it need not be the end. Instead it can be the start. Here are some ways that failure can help you.

Increase your motivation

"Minor setback? Major comeback" is a phrase often used by elite athletes. Although unpleasant at the time, failures often provide a strong boost to your motivation. The greatest basketball player of all time, Michael Jordan, once gave an insight into this when he said, "I have failed over and over and over again in my life. And that is why I succeed."

A learning opportunity

Some people are motivated by learning and mastering a subject, whereas others are more focused on rewards and comparing themselves to others.[28] Those from the first group are more likely to view setbacks as an opportunity to learn and improve. They see failure as a painful but valuable speed bump along the way. Furthermore, these people are more likely to be more confident and handle stressful situations better. Be in the first group, not the second.

Develop compassion

Recently researchers have found that people who have suffered setbacks show more compassion to others.[29] If you know how failure feels when you experience it, you are more likely to empathise with others when they experience setbacks. This skill is key to forming positive and healthy relationships with others.

Resilience and determination

Many Olympic champions have said that their resilience was a key skill needed to win their gold medals. Many of them have stated that their road to success has not been simple or straightforward, and that they have come to view the setbacks along the way as opportunities for growth.[30]

At the time of a setback, this can be difficult to appreciate, as emotions are often running high. This can cloud our judgement and impair learning. Once the dust has settled, ask yourself questions such as, "What would I do differently next time?" and "What have I learnt from this experience?"

Ask for help

It is a myth that asking for help is a sign of weakness. Nothing could be further from the truth. Jorgen Vig Knudstorp, former CEO of Lego, says "blame is not for failure, it is for failing to help or for asking for help." Asking for help from others and then using it well is a sign of strength. As Nobel Peace Prize winner Al Gore said in his acceptance speech, "If you want to go quickly, go alone. If you want to go far, go together."

Make the final achievement more rewarding

It takes years of experience, setbacks and practice to achieve one's dreams. Experiencing the lows can help you to appreciate your highs.

As has been said, "Success consists of going from failure to failure without loss of enthusiasm." Success at the end of the bumpy road often makes the hard times along the way all the more worth it.

7 Ways to Reduce the Fear of Failure

No Shame Policy
Be part of a group where failure isn't followed by laughter, ridicule and embarrassment.

Address the Problem
Don't be an ostrich and bury your head in the sand. What can you do to make the situation better?

Learn From Your Mistakes
Real failure is someone who has blundered and not cashed in on the experience.

Don't Bottle It Up
Talk to someone, like a parent or friend.

Question Your Fears
Are they actually irrational and highly unlikely to come true?

Focus on What You Can Control
A lot of the things you worry about are out of your hands and potentially down to chance.

Embrace the Grey
Success and failure shouldn't be seen as black or white. This all-or-nothing thinking can increase stress and anxiety.

REDUCING THE FEAR OF FAILURE

So if failure isn't always bad and can lead to increases of motivation, learning and determination, why are so many of us afraid of it? It turns out it is not failure that people fear, it is worrying about the negative consequences that might follow the failure that stresses us out. As Franklin D. Roosevelt said in his first presidential speech, "let me assert my firm belief that the only thing we have to fear is fear itself".

So how can you overcome the fear of failure? Here are some suggestions.

No shame

The most common fear associated with failure is the fear of shame and embarrassment.[31] This is why you might not ask questions in front of others for fear of looking stupid, or why some athletes play it too safe because they don't want to be the one who makes a mistake. Once you accept that failure is part of the learning process and that everyone makes mistakes, then you will start to be liberated from the fear of failure.

Address the problem

There are three ways that people cope with stress: 'avoidant focused', 'emotional focused' and 'problem focused'. Let's say you are worried about snakes in your garden. You could decide never to go into your garden again (avoidant focused), convince yourself that having snakes in your back garden isn't that bad (emotional focused) or go into your garden and get rid of them (problem focused).

You can see that avoidant and emotional focused coping strategies may provide some short term relief, but a problem focused coping strategy addresses the issue head on and allows you to make long term gains. Don't be an ostrich and bury your head in the sand. If something is worrying you, work out how you can make it better.

Learn from your mistakes

Forty years ago, a psychologist studied how people viewed an upcoming test. Some viewed it as an opportunity to see how much they had learnt; others saw it as a chance to compare themselves to their classmates.[32] It turns out that focusing more on your learning and individual development, instead of comparing yourself to others, improves long term motivation, confidence and academic performance as well as reducing anxiety.[33]

Question your fears

Author Mark Twain reportedly once commented that, "I've had a lot of worries in my life, most of which never happened." This quote perfectly captures how many people end up worrying about the worst case scenario, often for no logical reason. For the majority of the time, the worst case scenario hardly ever happens.

Focus on what you can control

When people focus on things that they can't change, it often makes them stressed or nervous. The opposite – focusing on what you can control – gives you a sense of certainty and confidence over a situation. Start by making a list of what you are thinking about. If you can't control it, don't waste too much time and energy on it. So remember: control the controllables.

Embrace the grey

It is easy to think that if the outcome is positive then everything leading up to it was good. On the other hand, if the outcome is negative then it is tempting to think that everything prior to it was bad. This sort of black and white thinking can lead to stress, anxiety and a fragile self-esteem. As well as judging yourself on the outcome, get the most from the grey. Judge yourself on your attitude, effort and most of all on what you have learnt from the journey.

7 Ways to Fail Better

"Ever tried. Ever failed. No matter. Try again. Fail again. Fail better."

After a failure, how many of these questions can you say yes to?

1 Were you trying something new?

2 Were you still motivated afterwards?

3 Was it the right thing to try at the time?

4 Did you ask for feedback?

5 Did you use the feedback you were given?

6 Have you reflected on the experience?

7 Are you clear on what you would do differently next time?

FAILING BETTER

Poet and playwright Samuel Beckett once wrote, "Ever tried. Ever failed. No matter. Try again. Fail again. Fail better." So how can you fail better? If you can answer yes to these questions, then you know you have had a 'good failure'.

Were you trying something new?

Being open and enthusiastic about new and challenging situations is a key characteristic of a successful mindset. Prior to the event, if your focus was on 'improving myself' instead of 'proving myself' then that is a worthy failure.

Were you still motivated after the setback?

It's not the fact but how you react that matters. Being truly successful in any activity is often more like a marathon than a sprint. To thrive in this environment your motivation needs to be robust and durable in order to aid resilience. Use your setbacks to add fuel to your motivational fire.

Was it the right thing to try at the time?

Nate Silver was the only man in the United States who correctly predicted how each of the 50 states would vote in the 2012 presidential election. He believes that instead of judging decisions based on the eventual outcome, it is far better to judge them based on the information you had at the time.[34]

If you made the best decision from the information you had at the time and still weren't successful, then perhaps the mistake was down to your execution of the skill and not the thought process that went into it. This is an important distinction to make as it can help you to identify which part of the process to target for improvement next time.

Did you ask for feedback (and then use it)?

Elbert Hubbard said, "A failure is a man who has blundered, but is not able to cash in the experience." Here is a three step method to ensure that you cash in on your experience and so fail better:

1   Actually ask someone for feedback.

2   Really listen to what they are saying and resist the temptation to get defensive.

3   Act on the feedback you have been given.

Common mistakes when asking for feedback include asking "Is this OK?" instead of "How can I make this better?", or asking too many questions at once which makes it harder to process all the answers you get given.

Then actively listen. There is no point in asking for feedback if you don't actually listen to how the person is trying to help you.

Finally, the whole feedback process means nothing unless you take some action as a result. It is not just enough to think about something or to have good intentions; it is the doing that really matters.

Did you reflect on the experience, and do you know what you would do differently next time?

Setbacks can aid the learning process but only if you take the time to reflect on what has happened, and as a result are clear on what you would do differently next time. Otherwise, it is likely that you will repeat the same mistakes again and again in the future. It is OK to make a mistake, but it is not OK to keep making the same one over and over again.

Asking yourself, "What would I do differently next time?" is a great question for two reasons. Firstly, it stops you dwelling on the past, which will make you feel better. Secondly, it looks towards the future positively as it focuses the mind on how to make the next outcome better. This will boost your confidence and motivation and help you to perform better.

6 Common Mistakes
When Asking for Feedback

1. Only asking "Is this OK?"

2. Not being fully present

3. Leaving it to the last moment

4. Asking 'either/or' questions

5. Asking multiple questions at once

6. Using superlatives – like 'always', 'never'

7 Ways to be More Optimistic

See setbacks as temporary
Viewing your setbacks as permanent makes you more likely to give up. See them as a learning curve and resolve to come back better because of them.

Regain a sense of control
What can you do to improve the situation? Focusing on this leads to more possible solutions, less problematic barriers and more action.

Don't over-generalise
After a disappointment, it is easy to think that everyone and everything is conspiring against you. Compartmentalise. A setback in one aspect of your life does not make you a failure in others.

Watch out for key phrases
Phrases such as "I will never", "I always mess up" and "This happens every time" after a failure are not helpful. Use phrases like "I might be able to" and "I could try this".

Shift your focus
It is tempting to focus on things you can't change. This can lead to stress and frustration as it is out of your hands. Control the controllables.

Take a balanced approach
Regardless of success or failure, there are always things that you did well and things you can do to improve. Build a stable base from which to learn.

Acknowledge your own contribution
Don't always put your success down to luck or other people performing worse than you. Build your optimism by reflecting on how you contributed to your successes.

CHAPTER 4

PERFORMING UNDER PRESSURE

DELIVER YOUR BEST WHEN IT MATTERS THE MOST

Flourishing vs. Wilting
Under Pressure

FLOURISHES   **WILTS**

- Believes they have the skills and resources
- The situation demands too much from them

- In control of the situation
- Not in control of the situation

- Feels supported
- Feels isolated

- What do I stand to gain?
- What do I stand to lose?

- Channels nerves in a helpful way
- Overwhelmed by nerves

- Reminds themselves of positive previous experiences
- Dwells on the uncertainty of what might happen

- Focuses on mastery, learning and getting better
- Worries about looking bad

- Believes they will achieve goals
- Thinks they won't achieve goals

- Throws themselves into the task at hand
- Disengages and withdraws

- Makes clear and decisive decisions
- Makes confused decisions

Based on research by @DrMJTurner and @DrJamieBarker

FLOURISHING VS. WILTING

Pressure is an interesting thing. It makes some people nervous, which often leads to them making sloppy mistakes and underperforming. For others, pressure improves their concentration and determination. They focus their efforts and, as a result, perform to the best of their abilities.

So what separates those who flourish from those who wilt under pressure? Scientists have been examining this question for a long time. Their findings suggest that how you perceive a situation can impact on how you think, feel and perform during it.[35] If it is your interpretation that matters, then that means that how you react to pressure is your choice.

Challenge vs. threat

You can interpret an event as either a challenge or a threat. Those who react well under pressure are said to be in the 'challenge state' whereas those who don't are in the 'threat state'. The challenge state is associated with an increase in adrenaline, whereas the threat state is associated with an increase in the stress hormone cortisol.[36]

People in the threat state tend to feel quite isolated. They are likely to focus on what they stand to lose if they are unsuccessful and they worry about what will happen if it all goes wrong. They think people are judging them and tend to stress about making a mistake. For most, this does not make them feel better and is likely to lead to a worse performance.

The threat state leads to people feeling overwhelmed by nerves, worrying about looking bad and believing that their goals are unobtainable. As a result, they make muddled and confused decisions and even disengage from the task at hand. This thought process leads to them having regrets and not fully expressing themselves and their talents.

So how do you get yourself into the challenge state? The key to this is to develop the skills and resources to meet the situation and believe you can do so. It also helps to surround yourself with supportive people and to focus on what you can control.

Other techniques to nudge yourself towards a challenge state include reminding yourself of previous situations that have gone well and how you have successfully overcome adversity in the past.[37] This boost to your confidence and resilience will result in you throwing yourself into the task and making clear and decisive decisions.

6 Ways to Improve Confidence

USING THE PAST

1 Remind yourself of previous success.

2 Remind yourself of your preparation.

USING THE NOW

3 Talk to yourself in a positive, helpful and energised way.

4 Seek out similar people who have been successful.

USING THE FUTURE

5 Visualise yourself being successful.

6 Know that setbacks today can help you develop skills needed for tomorrow.

HOW TO IMPROVE YOUR CONFIDENCE

No other quality is as elusive and yet so important to your performance as confidence. Everyone knows they need it to perform at their best, but most would struggle to know what strategies to use to increase their self-confidence.

For some, confidence is a fragile thing. This is especially true for those who base it on just one source, be it the opinion or approval of one individual or how you did in your last performance. There are many strategies that can make you feel confident, utilising the past, present and future. Here are some you could try.

Using the past

Remind yourself of previous success

A key component of how confident you feel on a particular task is whether you have successfully completed a similar task in the past.[38] This reminds you that you have the abilities and the resources needed to meet the challenge.

Remind yourself of your preparation

Your preparation can be a source of confidence.[39] If you have put in the work leading up to an event, then remind yourself of this. Sources of confidence that are within your control are far more enduring than those that are out of your control.[40]

Using the present

Talk to yourself in a positive, helpful and energised way

How you talk to yourself can affect how you think, feel and subsequently perform. Self-talk is more than just talking to yourself in a positive way ("I can do this"). In addition, try talking to yourself in a helpful way ("I need to do X, Y, Z in order to do well")[41] and also in an energised way ("Come on, keep going").[42]

Seek out similar people who have been successful

Can you think of anyone else who has achieved what you are about to try? Remind yourself of others who have been successful in similar tasks. This will help to increase your self-confidence, as you are providing evidence to your brain that the task is achievable. It is not impossible, and if others can do it then you can as well.

Using the future

Visualise yourself being successful

Picturing yourself doing well can help to improve your mood, reduce your nerves[43] and also increase your confidence.[44] As well as seeing yourself achieve the outcome you want, it is also helpful to visualise the behaviours and skills you will need in order to achieve that success. It is important to note that this technique can lead to some people daydreaming about future success, so be sure to use it only just prior to the event and only if you have already put in the hard work during your preparation phase.

Know that setbacks today can help you develop skills needed for tomorrow

Setbacks, though painful at the time, can actually help in the long run. Knowing that failure is not fatal and can lead to you learning and developing will help to reduce the fear of failure.

6 Ways to Talk to Yourself

Say "Stop"

Saying "Stop" straight after a negative thought helps people manage frustrations, overcome nerves, sleep better and not dwell on the worst case scenario.

Ask Questions

By asking yourself "How am I going to do this?" your brain starts to generate potential answers.
This means you start focusing on solutions and not dwelling on the problem.

Give Yourself Instructions

Telling yourself what to do focuses attention, helps you learn new tasks quicker and helps you perform more consistently under pressure.

Energising Language

Talk to yourself in an energising way. This can increase your motivation, effort and endurance as well as keeping potential distractions at bay.

Second Person

In studies, those who give themselves instructions in the first person ('I') perform worse than those who give themselves advice in the second person ('You').

Positive People

Surround yourself with positive people. Researchers have found that negative statements made by teachers were predictive of how negatively boys talked to themselves.

WAYS TO IMPROVE HOW YOU TALK TO YOURSELF

How well you talk to yourself impacts on how you feel and, subsequently, how well you perform. Your self-talk will affect your persistence, concentration and stress levels. Here are simple techniques that will help you talk to yourself in a better way.

Say "Stop"

Saying stop straight after a negative thought helps you to manage frustration, overcome nerves, sleep better and stop dwelling on worst case scenarios.[45] You may not be able to control the first thing that pops into your head, but you can control the second. Saying stop is a good strategy that allows you to take control of your inner voice and acts as a springboard to move on to more helpful thoughts.

Ask yourself questions

This is especially effective when adopting a new behaviour or when you are in an unfamiliar scenario as it prompts you to think through the problem.[46] Actress and United Nations Women Goodwill Ambassador, Emma Watson, used this technique to good effect before giving a speech to UN delegates on the importance of equal rights for all. At the start her voice cracked and she appeared palpably nervous. However, she carried on and delivered a powerful and moving speech.

What did she say to herself to deal with those nerves? As she says during her talk, "In my nervousness for this speech and in my moments of doubt I told myself firmly – if not me, who? If not now, when? If you have similar doubts when opportunities are presented to you I hope those words might be helpful."[47]

Give yourself instructions

Telling yourself what to do, instead of just saying that you are going to do well, can be a very effective way to talk to yourself. As artist Vincent van Gogh said, "If you hear a voice within you saying, 'You are not a painter,' then by all means paint ... and that voice will be silenced." This technique helps athletes to improve their concentration whilst under pressure,[48] as well as helping students to improve their self-control in the classroom, as it helps you plan and prepare more effectively.[49]

Energising language

Talking to yourself in an upbeat manner can increase your motivation – an approach adopted by many when they tell themselves to 'keep going' when running on a treadmill. This type of self-talk can also help to block out potentially distracting thoughts and aid self-control, especially for tasks that require large amounts of effort and energy.[50] It is also helpful if the people around you have a positive outlook as this affects how you talk to yourself.[51]

'You' is better than 'I'

Talking to yourself in the second person (i.e. "You can do this") is more effective than talking to yourself in the first person (i.e. "I can do this"). In a public speaking test, researchers stressed out participants by telling them they had to give a speech in front of judges in order to win their ideal job.[52] Half of the participants were instructed to talk to themselves in the first person ('I') and the other half with the word 'you'. The results? Those who used 'you' reported feeling more confident and less nervous than those who used 'I'. Interestingly, the judges also viewed them as having made a better first impression.

IMPROVING METACOGNITION

Metacognition is the term used to describe how aware you are of what you are thinking about and your ability to then take control of your thoughts. This is a key component of performing under pressure. Metacognition is a skill that, like any other, can and should be developed over time. Developing this skill has been shown to help students improve their performance in school.[53]

In order to learn how to develop this skill, let's look at how metacognition can be applied in three time periods: before the task, during the task and after the task.

This 'before, during, after' approach is very similar to the 'plan, do, review' mantra which is used in elite sport. By breaking the task down into before, during and after, you ensure that you are fully prepared before, on the right track during and learning as much as possible afterwards.

Here are nine simple questions that you should ask yourself to help develop your metacognitive skills.

9 Questions to Improve Metacognition

Before

▶ Is this similar to a previous task?

▶ What do I want to achieve?

▶ What should I do first?

During

▶ Am I on the right track?

▶ What can I do differently?

▶ Who can I ask for help?

After

▶ What worked well?

▶ What could I have done better?

▶ Can I apply this to other situations?

Before a task

1 Is this similar to a previous task?

2 What do I want to achieve?

3 What should I do first?

These questions will remind you of times when you have done similar tasks. This will help you to remember how you successfully went about the task. Asking "What do I want to achieve?" means you will have a clear objective, and "What should I do first?" means you start off on the right foot.

During the task

4 Am I on the right track?

5 What can I do differently?

6 Who can I ask for help?

These questions allow you to monitor your progress and tweak your approach. It is important in any task to have a certain degree of flexibility. As martial artist Bruce Lee once commented, "the stiffest tree is easily cracked under pressure, but the bamboo survives by bending with the wind".

After a task

7 What worked well?

8 What could I have done better?

9 Can I apply this to other situations?

After a task it is tempting to get obsessed about the outcome. If you achieve everything then you think all is good. If you fail then everything must have been bad. Neither of these extreme views is likely to prompt the much needed self-reflection that spurs on improvement. Asking both "What worked well?" and "What could I have done better?", regardless of the outcome, ensures a healthy, balanced approach to both success and failure.

6 Ways to Manage Self-Doubt

1. **Know That a Little Bit of Self-Doubt Is Good**

2. **Weigh Up the Evidence**

3. **Write Down Your Nerves**

4. **Don't Sweat the Small Stuff**

5. **Be Kind to Yourself**

6. **Focus on Your Preparation**

HOW TO CONQUER SELF-DOUBT

Everyone has moments of self-doubt. As William Shakespeare wrote in *Measure for Measure*, "Our doubts are traitors, and make us lose the good we oft might win, by fearing to attempt." For some, these thoughts are fleeting and quickly pass. For others, as Shakespeare suggests, they can have a more debilitating effect. Self-doubt is a place where many meander but few flourish. So what simple things can you do to manage self-doubt?

A little bit of self-doubt is good

Self-doubt isn't always a bad thing; in fact, a little self-doubt may cause us to put in more effort.[54] If you have too much confidence it makes you underestimate the task at hand, meaning you put in less effort.[55] A bit of self-doubt that is followed by action can be really helpful.

Weigh up the evidence

Weighing up the evidence — by challenging how logical and rational your doubts are — is a great technique to use. Irrational thoughts can lead to increased anxiety. Practise recognising which thoughts are unhelpful and then replacing them with more accurate and helpful ones.

Write down your nerves

When you become anxious about an upcoming event, these worries can disrupt your focus on the current task.[56] Writing about your worries helps to combat self-doubt. By getting your concerns down on paper, you are addressing, making sense and eliminating them before you even perform. This will free you to have better focus and attention on the upcoming event.

Don't sweat the small stuff

Your worries and doubts tend to make the situation seem far worse than it actually is. How often do you look back on an issue a couple of months later and think, "Why did I worry so much about that?" So, instead of exaggerating your doubts, try to be more realistic and see the concern as a minor obstacle.

Be kind to yourself

Try these tips: be kind to yourself when you fail, recognise that everyone fails at some stage, focus on the bigger picture and acknowledge that it is unreasonable to expect yourself never to make a mistake. Chapter 8 goes into more detail on this subject.

Focus on your preparation

Focusing on your preparation helps you to concentrate on what you can control. Being fully prepared means you can stop focusing on the unwanted distractions which can chip away at your self-belief. Preparation doesn't guarantee success, but it certainly increases the chances of it.

CHAPTER 5

MAKE YOUR LEARNING STICK

MAXIMISE YOUR REVISION

GOOD REVISERS

POOR REVISERS

Good Revisers		Poor Revisers
Eat breakfast		Skip breakfast
Sleep 8–10 hours a night		Get little sleep
Have regular bedtimes		Have inconsistent bedtimes
Get fresh air each day		Stay indoors all day
Exercise regularly		Do no exercise
Do past papers		Mostly revise highlighting 'key' passages
Spread out their revision		Cram their revision
Keep a diary to capture negative thoughts		Dwell on worst case scenarios
Revise in a quiet environment		Revise whilst listening to music or TV
Drink water regularly		Forget to stay hydrated
Put their phone away during revision		Revise with their mobile phone next to them

GOOD VS. POOR REVISERS

We now know more about the science of learning than ever before. There are some really simple things you can do whilst revising to improve your memory, mood and concentration. Here's how ...

Eat breakfast

It is estimated that over 60% of teenage boys and 70% of teenage girls regularly skip breakfast.[57] Eating breakfast, especially cereals rich in complex carbohydrates, helps to boost your concentration and memory over the course of the morning.[58]

Get fresh air and do some exercise

Taking a break in a field or park will improve your concentration. Students report a 20% improvement in their performance on a boring task if they have taken a break outside in natural surroundings.[59] It also helps to do some exercise too. Researchers have found that people perform significantly better if they exercise for 45 minutes at lunchtime. As well as improving their mood and ability to deal with stressful situations, their scores for their concentration levels were 21% higher.[60]

Ditch the highlighters

Despite being one of the most popular revision strategies, using highlighters is one of the least effective.[61] Most people tend to overuse them, making it more akin to colouring in than to effective highlighting. If you really want to use highlighters, only highlight the key parts of the text that really matter and try not to have too many categories. If you are highlighting with more colours than the colours of the rainbow, then you are doing it wrong.

Don't listen to music

Music can have a positive impact in some situations: it can help to improve your motivation and enhance your mood. However, when it comes to learning new material, processing it and recalling that information later, it is easy for music to get in the way.

Students who revise listening to music have been found to be able to recall less than those who revise in a quiet environment.[62] Music with no lyrics is better than music with lyrics, regardless of whether you like the lyrics or not. That is because processing music takes up some of your brain's capacity, leaving fewer resources available for you to recall the information you are trying to remember.

Drink water regularly

Drinking water has been shown to help improve both memory and concentration.[63] Don't wait until you feel thirsty; by this stage your concentration levels will already have dropped. Sipping water regularly can help to ensure your focus stays sharp and your attention levels stay high.

Put your phone away

Having your phone out and in sight, even if you aren't using it, can make you perform 20% worse than if you had put your phone away.[64] The implication couldn't be clearer: out of sight really is out of mind.

8 Ways to
Work Smarter

For Revision To Be Effective You Must ...

1 Target a specific part of your knowledge

2 Take yourself out of your comfort zone

3 Reinforce and build on previous work

4 Get feedback on what you are doing

5 Strengthen your weaknesses

6 Build on your strengths

7 Put in the hard work and intensity

8 Give it your full focus and concentration

HOW TO WORK SMARTER

The Greek philosopher Aristotle believed that we are what we repeatedly do, so excellence is not an act but a habit. During revision, many students confuse how hard they are working with how well they are working. For revision to be effective, you need to work both hard and smart.

Why do some people improve and learn at a faster rate than others? Answering this question has been researcher K. Anders Ericsson's life work.[65] He has studied expert performers in nearly every walk of life – be it chess, music, sport or business. He found that experts in these very different areas shared one thing in common: they didn't just work hard, they worked smart. They used their time developing their skills effectively. The following tips provide a handy checklist to ensure that you do the same whilst revising.

Target a specific part of your knowledge

Imagine you are practising a song on an instrument and struggle with the middle section. Would it be better to practise the whole song through or focus on the part you struggle with? The answer is definitely the latter. The same is true no matter what the task. Focus on the specific parts that you want to work on. The more time you spend practising and developing specific gaps in your knowledge, the better they will become.

Take yourself out of your comfort zone

Stretching yourself means trying to improve by an amount that is just possible if you push yourself. This often means choosing the slightly more difficult question or spending time on areas that you haven't quite mastered yet.

Reinforce and build on previous work

A random scattergun approach is unlikely to yield long term gains. Being able to link to and build on previous revision sessions will help to solidify information in your long term memory. This is called 'scaffolding' as it literally helps you to build on previous experiences.

A good approach to revision is to spend some time at the start reminding yourself of what you have learnt previously. After that, do your current revision before finally reflecting on how this new content relates to and develops your previous knowledge.

Get feedback on what you are doing

Feedback is the guide that you need to follow to better your abilities. If you don't get feedback on what you are doing, how can you know for sure that you are getting better at it? Test yourself as you go along.

Strengthen your weaknesses and build on your strengths

Left to our own devices, many people will spend their time on what they are good at, which is normally the subjects they enjoy the most. It is important to build on your strengths because settling for good is often the enemy of great. However, nothing develops confidence and motivation more than improving, and your weaknesses offer the greatest scope for this. So be sure to do both: strengthen your weaknesses *and* build on your strengths.

Put in the hard work and give it your full concentration

It is hard to achieve anything significant without hard work, commitment and concentration. Working hard doesn't guarantee success, but it makes it a lot more likely.

15 ways
to Improve Memory

Write things down

Chunking

KISS BTW OMG
S.C.U.B.A.
Acronyms

Practice, practice, practice

Superior focus

Test yourself

Silly sentences

Teach it to someone else

Drink water

Read more

Little and often

Make it a story

Blah, bla
ah, blah,...

Say things out loud

Ask why

Get enough sleep

MAXIMISING YOUR MEMORY

Working around your working memory

On average, humans can hold around seven things in their working memory.[66] One way to overcome this is to write things down. By doing this we don't have to juggle lots of information in our working memory; we can store it on a piece of paper and refer back to it when we need it.

Sometimes it isn't possible to write things down. In these situations, techniques such as chunking, acronyms and silly sentences can help. Chunking is when small bits of information are grouped together. For example, it is much easier to remember a number sequence like '0, 7, 1, 0, 1, 9, 8, 4' when it is chunked into three groups (i.e. in a calendar format) like this: '07, 10, 1984'.

An acronym is where each letter in a word acts as a cue to remember something else. For example, scuba is actually a shortcut for self-contained underwater breathing apparatus, and SOHCAHTOA is an acronym used in maths to work out the dimensions of a triangle.

Silly sentences work in a similar way, with the first letter of each word acting as a reminder for another word. One example of this is the sentence: "Richard of York gave battle in vain." It's a handy way of remembering the colours of the rainbow: red, orange, yellow, green, blue, indigo, violet.

Long term memory

When revising, it is more effective to space out your study sessions rather than cramming at the last minute. Spacing out revision is good as it leaves you with enough time to forget and relearn.[67] This process helps you to cement knowledge in your memory. Actors don't leave all their rehearsals until the day before the opening night of a play. Athletes don't only train the day before the match. Committing something to memory takes time.

It is far better to revise for one hour a day for eight days rather than cram eight hours of revision into one day.

If you are revising with someone else, it is good to take turns teaching each other the material.[68] This helps because teaching someone else requires you to learn and recall information in a clear and organised way.

When you learn the material, be sure to test yourself too. This is the most effective strategy to use during revision. Testing yourself with past papers, short quizzes or having someone ask you questions forces you to think deeply about the material, which improves the chance of it being stored in your long term memory.[69]

Another good technique to improve memory is to ask yourself "Why?" One study investigating this asked three groups of students to remember a list of sentences (e.g. "The hungry man got into the car").[70] The first group simply read the sentence, the second group was given an explanation (i.e. to go to a restaurant) and the third group was asked to come up with their own reason why the man got in his car. The results? Students from the third group who were prompted to ask why remembered twice as many sentences as the other two groups.

Once you have spaced out your learning, repeated it out loud, taught it to someone else, tested yourself and asked why, all you have left to do is repeat it again and again. Don't stop once you get it right. Keep practising until you never get it wrong.

5 Ways to Make the Most of Your Revision Time

Space Out Your Learning

Don't leave everything to the last minute. Start early and revisit topics regularly. This will help keep information in your long term memory.

Create a Sense of Purpose

Telling yourself how learning the material will help you achieve your future goals can help create a sense of purpose and keep you motivated.

Test Yourself

Research suggests that this is one of the most effective ways to improve your memory. It can help prepare you for exam conditions.

Sleep Well

Sleep plays a major role in how you feel and how much you remember. Don't neglect getting a good night's sleep. Regular routines such as consistent bedtimes and wake-up times will help.

Teach It

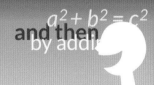

By teaching the material to someone else, it can help ensure you fully understand the main concepts with clarity.

CREATING A SENSE OF PURPOSE

How well motivated you are plays a key part in how well you do something. The greatest boxer of all time, Muhammad Ali, was known for training hard. His coach, Angelo Dundee, said, "He was always the first guy in the gym and the last to leave." Ali himself once said, "I hated every minute of training, but I said, 'Don't quit. Suffer now and live the rest of your life as a champion.'" He was a man on a mission and knew that the more he sweated in training, the less he would bleed in battle.

This powerful technique of reminding yourself how the task will benefit you in the future is known as 'creating a sense of purpose'. For example, a recent study examined how students best learnt new material.[72] They were divided into four groups:

Group 1 were not given any reason as to why they should do the task.

Group 2 were told they should try hard as it was expected of them.

Group 3 were told to pay attention as they would have to take a test at the end.

Group 4 were told it would help them in their future career.

The result? Group 4 put in much more effort and learnt more than the other three groups because they had a sense of purpose. They knew what their 'why' was. Working out what your why is will increase your motivation, and coupled with effective revision strategies it will help you to learn and remember your key revision notes more effectively.

Beat Revision Stress

1
Do the actual work – revise!

2
When really stressed, talk to someone about it

3
Get some fresh air each day

4
Stick to regular mealtimes

5
Do something to switch off an hour before bed

6
Don't dwell on worst case scenarios

7
A good sleep the night before is better than last minute cramming

8
Once you've done the exam, move on to the next one

9
Don't aim for perfection – it's a myth and doesn't exist

HOW TO MANAGE REVISION STRESS

Revision time is one of the most stressful periods of the year for many students. These stress levels can badly impact your memory and can make you feel frustrated and anxious. So, as well as improving memory and motivation, it is important to be kind and look after yourself during revision. These tips will help to nudge you in the right direction.

Do the actual work – revise!

You don't need to post about how much revising you are doing on Facebook, Instagram or Twitter. You don't need to delay any longer by making your revision timetable pretty and colour coordinated. You do need to do the revision. Address the problem head on and don't procrastinate any longer. The dragon is never as big as you imagine. By starting the battle you will feel better for it.

When really stressed, talk to someone about it

Talking through your problems, fears or worries can be very therapeutic. Parents, teachers and older siblings have experience in managing the stress of revision and exams; talking to them, even if they don't have all the answers, can help you gain clarity in your own mind about what you need to do next. Likewise, friends who are going through the same stresses may be able to offer useful advice.

Get some fresh air each day

A recent report found that many people spend less time outside each day than prisoners.[73] The value of nature shouldn't be underestimated – those who spend more time outside feel better and calmer.[74] It has also been proven that getting fresh air helps to improve your concentration when you come back to your work.[75]

Stick to regular mealtimes

Regular mealtimes help you to structure your day. This consistency provides a great platform to plan your revision around. In addition, it can help to improve your mood, as those who regularly skip meals (especially break-fast) report being far more stressed over the course of the day.[76]

Do something to switch off an hour before bed

Is your bedtime routine helping or hindering you getting to sleep? One of the best ways to fall asleep is to go to bed relaxed. If you are stressed this will be difficult. Make sure that the last hour before bed is spent unwinding from the day's revision and not spent revising.

Don't dwell on worst case scenarios

Under the stress of exams it is easy to catastrophise and assume the worst case scenario. How do you overcome this? Look for alternative evidence and don't talk in extremes or superlatives (e.g. 'always', 'have to', 'every time'). It is really important to challenge these unhelpful and negative thoughts.

Don't sacrifice a good night's sleep for last minute cramming

Cramming is a poor revision strategy. It is particularly poor if it means missing out on valuable sleep. Not getting enough sleep hinders your concentration, mood, memory and judgement, and so should be actively avoided.

Once you've done the exam, move on to the next one

People naturally have a negative bias – that is to say, they are more likely to remember the bad stuff over the good. By overthinking the exam once you have finished it, it is tempting to work yourself up into a state as you dwell on the one or two questions you think you got wrong. Don't ask too many people what they put down for each answer, as this will probably do more harm than good. Just focus on your preparation for the next exam.

CHAPTER 6

EXCELLENCE IN EXAMS

GET THE GRADES YOU DESERVE

THE BENEFITS OF MOCK EXAMS

Taking mock exams and practising past papers is a key part of excellent preparation for your exams. If you can see them as an opportunity, then you are more likely to maximise their value. This will help make sure you are on the path to exam success. Here are some ways that mock exams help.

7 Ways That Mocks Are Good For You

1. Motivate you to do revision early

2. Help you identify topics you need to revise

3. Test effective revision strategies

4. You can get used to exam pressure

5. Allow you to practise exam techniques

6. Increase belief that exams are doable

7. Are an opportunity to ask for help

Overcome procrastination

Mock exams can help you to overcome procrastination by prompting you to start your revision early. Spacing out your revision and doing a little and often, instead of a lot at the last minute, is the best revision strategy.[77] Taking your mock exams seriously provides an opportunity for you to focus your attention and efforts earlier.

Better revision, better exam performance

The act of being tested enhances memory and future exam performance. In a study on mock exams, researchers found that students who did a practice test after a period of revision did better in the final exam than those students who didn't do the mock exam and had just spent the whole time revising.[78]

Identifying topics that need attention

Mock exam results can help you identify how best to spend the coming months. Once these areas are identified, it is then a case of putting in the hours. It is not enough to think about what you need to do better; it is the action and the doing that really makes the difference.

Shock in the mock

Instead of seeing a mock exam as an inconvenience, view it as a chance to really test your knowledge. It is better to do the work and find out where the gaps in your knowledge are when there are no major consequences. The shock in the mock is a springboard for success; a slam in the final exam is not.

Practise under exam conditions

Mock exams offer the opportunity to practise under exam conditions. Having a trial run reduces the stress surrounding your final exam as you will know more about what to expect. If your final exams are the first time you experience pressurised exam conditions, it will be a lottery as you will not know how to react.

7 Things to Think About
the Night Before an Exam

1 POSITIVE IMAGERY
Spend some time visualising a positive
exam experience. This will increase your
confidence, help with nerves and enhance your mood.

2 YOUR BEST PERFORMANCE
Think about a previous good performance.
What helped you do well that time and how
will you apply that tomorrow?

3 YOUR PREPARATION
Boost your confidence by reminding
yourself of how well you have prepared
and how much revision you have done.

4 FOCUS ON YOU
Focus on yourself and don't compare yourself
to others as this will make you feel stressed.
Instead, focus on what you can control.

5 THE CHALLENGE
If you see the exam as a threat, it will make
you stressed. View the exam as an opportunity
or as a challenge. This will make you feel better.

6 OVERCOMING SETBACKS
Remind yourself how you overcame previous setbacks.
This will help you deal with future challenges
and build mental resilience.

7 A GOOD NIGHT'S SLEEP
A good night's sleep helps improve creativity,
problem solving, concentration and memory.
This is more important than last minute cramming

6 Tips for the Morning of an Exam

 Eat breakfast as this will help fuel your brain

 Arrive at school with plenty of time

 Avoid people who stress you out

 Remind yourself of all the hard work and preparation you have put in

 Feeling nervous? Pause for a minute and take some deep breaths

 Remind yourself of your exam strategy

THE MORNING OF AN EXAM

Having spent so much effort revising for an exam, it is careless to leave the last hour or two to chance. It is not enough to have knowledge in order to do well; often you have to demonstrate this knowledge under some pressure. This is why what you do in the hours building up to your exam matters.

Expert performers in all walks of life have pre-performance routines for that very reason. This is true for actors before a play, musicians before a concert and athletes before a competition.[79] So why not use the same techniques before your exam? The strategies below give you the best chance of demonstrating your knowledge when it really matters.

Eat breakfast and leave early

Breakfast provides the fuel you need for the day. Just like a car can't run on empty, neither can your body or your brain. Once you have eaten breakfast, plan to leave your house with plenty of time so you are not rushing to get to school. Exams are stressful enough without the added worry of running late. Lateness tends to magnify everything; if you are a bit stressed or nervous, you will be more so if you are running late. Follow the old maxim, "If you're not early, you're late," and you'll be on the right path to starting your exams calmly and confidently.

Avoid people who stress you out

It has been said that you are the average of the five people you spend the most time with. Attitude is contagious.[80] Is the mindset of those you currently spend your time with worth catching? On the morning of an exam, think about who makes you feel calm and confident and actively seek them out. Avoid spending the time before your exam surrounded by people who are particularly negative or who stress you out.

Pause for a minute and take some deep breaths

When people are under pressure they often underestimate how much time they have. This leads to them rushing and making careless mistakes that cost marks. Taking a few deep breaths can act as a prompt to slow you down. Physiologically this helps to lower your heart rate and reduce tension. By slowing down or pausing for a moment, you give yourself time to fully assess the situation, come up with a plan and decide the best course of action.

Remind yourself of your exam strategy

American football coach Bill Walsh wrote in his book, *The Score Takes Care of Itself*, that his approach was to focus on executing a game strategy and not to worry about the goal tally.[81] If you do this, he said, the result will often take care of itself.

The same is true during exams. Focus less on what grade you might get and more on executing your exam strategy. This might mean thinking about the amount of time you spend on each question, reading each question twice before writing, jotting down five minutes of rough notes before answering the long question or using the other techniques you have learnt from your teachers during your exam preparation. If you are not sure what your exam strategy should be, ask your teacher; they will almost certainly have some helpful advice for you.

7 Ways to [STOP] Panic
Taking Over During an Exam

1. TAKE SOME DEEP BREATHS
This will help clear your head and give you time to think.

2. RE-READ THE QUESTION
This will help ensure you don't misread the question
and you avoid making sloppy mistakes.

3. THINK BACK TO YOUR REVISION
Have you answered similar questions previously during your revision?

4. WHAT WOULD YOUR TEACHER SAY?
What advice would your teacher give you to help you right now?

5. SOMETHING IS BETTER THAN NOTHING
Better to guess the answer than leave it blank. If you don't write
anything down you are guaranteed to get zero marks.

6. STICK TO YOUR EXAM STRATEGY
If you have a bad first question, stick to your pre-planned strategy and
don't let the bad start affect your performance on the next question.

7. DON'T PUT TOO MUCH PRESSURE ON YOURSELF
Work your hardest and do your best. Some stress is good but
becoming too stressed doesn't help you think clearly under pressure.

HANDLING EXAM PRESSURE

Some people are naturally good at controlling their emotions, whereas others have to work a bit harder at it. It is important to know that the ability to manage your nerves is something that can be learnt. If you get nervous in exams, try one of these strategies to help you perform at your best.

Take some deep breaths

When under pressure, your brain becomes awash with hormones such as adrenaline and cortisol. In many cases, this makes people speed up, as they think they have less time left than they actually do. If you pause for a moment and take a deep breath, everything slows down and it helps you to refocus.[82]

Read the question twice – without holding your pen

One of the most frequent mistakes made in an exam is to misread the question. Re-reading a question sounds so simple, but it's amazing how easy it is for concentration to lapse momentarily. If you know that you are a bit impatient or have misread questions in the past, try putting your pen down when you read the question. This will help counteract the urge to rush and write down an answer immediately.

Think back to your revision

Have you answered similar questions before? Even if you haven't faced this exact question before, remembering a successful thought process can help to get you started. This is because it helps you to be aware of your thought processes and select an effective way of thinking about a problem, rather than panicking. As we saw in Chapter 4, this way of thinking about your thinking (metacognition) has been found to be one of the most effective strategies for improving performance.[83]

What would your teacher say?

Chances are that over the previous months your teachers will have repeatedly given advice and suggestions on how best to go about answering a question. When you come under stress, asking "What would my teacher say?" should help you to get back on track. During the stress of the exam, it is sometimes difficult to see the wood for the trees. Taking a moment to pause and think about what advice your teacher would give allows you to create a space around you to help you think more clearly.

Something is better than nothing

Write nothing at all and you are guaranteed to get zero. You might as well write something down. This is called 'a shot to nothing', as you have nothing to lose if it goes wrong. Legendary ice hockey player Wayne Gretzky echoed this sentiment when he said, "You miss 100% of the shots you don't take."

Don't put too much pressure on yourself

Some stress can help aid performance, but excessive pressure often stops people from thinking clearly. Be kind to yourself in the exam. This can be done by using words and phrases such as 'sometimes', 'I could' or 'I might', instead of 'every time', 'I should' or 'I must'. Too much pressure on yourself can lead to perfectionism, which hinders instead of helps you.

CHAPTER 7

SLEEP YOUR WAY TO SUCCESS

SLEEP TIGHT, THINK RIGHT

6 Benefits of a Good Night's Sleep

Better Concentration

Better Memory and Recall

Aids Creativity

Helps You Make Better Decisions

Reduced Focus on Negative Things

Stronger Immune System

THE BENEFITS OF A GOOD NIGHT'S SLEEP

In the quest for excellence, getting enough sleep is often the lowest priority. This is a particularly poor choice. People who get a regular good night's sleep think, feel and perform better. For example, people who don't get enough sleep are more likely to get ill,[84] make worse decisions and have lower levels of memory and concentration.[85] Furthermore, sleep duration and quality have a significant impact on exam performance,[86] with students who regularly get a good night's sleep achieving higher grades than their sleepier peers.[87]

Most people don't get enough sleep, with many teenagers getting less than seven hours a night.[88] How much sleep do you need? It depends on your age. Teenagers need more than adults, with GCSE and sixth form students requiring up to ten hours a night and adults around eight on average.[89]

9 Common Sleep Mistakes

1 Watching TV right up until bedtime

2 Long naps in the day

3 Killing time online

4 Different bedtimes each night

5 Drinking tea, coffee, cola or energy drinks late at night

6 Waiting to fall asleep before going to bed

7 Being on your phone in bed

8 Staying in bed when unable to sleep

9 Overthinking tomorrow

COMMON SLEEP MISTAKES

The chances are that you are not getting enough sleep. Despite sleeping for an average of 20 years during their lifetime, a lot of people are not doing it right. The musician Adele almost got excluded from school for continually turning up late. She said, "I wasn't doing anything. I wasn't bunking. I just couldn't wake up."[90]

These are the nine most common sleep mistakes you need to avoid.

Watching TV right up until bedtime

Watching TV is the most common reported activity before bed and often results in people going to sleep later than they otherwise would have.[91] The temptation is to stay awake and watch junk TV at the expense of a good night's sleep. Identify junk TV by asking yourself this question: if I wouldn't get up an hour earlier tomorrow morning to watch this, why am I staying up an hour later to watch it?

Napping for too long

If you nap for too long or too late in the evening, it can start a vicious cycle where you stay up late into the night, don't get enough sleep and so wake up tired. This results in you having to nap the next afternoon or evening, and so the cycle continues.

Spending hours online killing time even when tired

If your body is tired, it means it is telling you to go to sleep. Don't waste time doing things that aren't important. Videos of baby pandas sneezing on YouTube will still be there tomorrow.

Different bedtimes each night

Different bedtimes each night confuse your body's internal clock and disrupt your sleep patterns. It is difficult to get a consistent night's sleep with an inconsistent routine.

Drinking tea, coffee or energy drinks late at night

These sorts of drinks are high in caffeine which increases your alertness. They often take at least 20 minutes to kick in, meaning that if you drink them before bed, you will feel more awake at the exact time you want to be falling asleep.

Waiting to fall asleep before going to bed

Have you tried the pillow test? If you fall asleep within five minutes of your head hitting the pillow, then you probably aren't getting enough sleep. If you find yourself consistently falling asleep on the sofa, it is a good indicator that you need to go to bed earlier.

Being on your phone in bed

The sleep hormone melatonin gets released when it is dark. If you are on your phone or tablet in bed, the bright light from the device fools your brain into thinking it is day and stops melatonin from being fully released, keeping you wide awake.[92]

Staying in bed when unable to sleep

If you can't fall asleep within 20–30 minutes, get out of bed and do something that occupies your brain without stressing it out. It is easy to get tense and frustrated when you want to be asleep but can't nod off. This makes you less likely to then fall asleep. Do something calming like reading a book.

Overthinking tomorrow

When in bed, it is tempting to overthink what you have to do the following day. It is easy to fall into the trap of dwelling on the possible consequences of it all going wrong. This can make you stressed, keeping you awake late into the night. It's good to know that worst case scenarios hardly ever happen. Things often seem better in the morning.

6 SCIENTIFICALLY PROVEN
WAYS TO HELP YOU FALL ASLEEP

REGULAR BEDTIMES/WAKE TIMES
Keeps your body clock consistent and helps you avoid distractions.

Bedtime

EXERCISE FOR AN HOUR A DAY
Exercise tires you out, increases the blood flow in your arteries and raises your body temperature.

Bedtime -2 hrs

TURN DOWN BRIGHTNESS OF YOUR PHONE
The sleep hormone melatonin gets released when it is dark. The bright light on your phone stops this happening.

Bedtime -2 hrs

EAT A TURKEY AND CHEESE SANDWICH
Turkey, cheese and bread all contain tryptophan, which helps you fall asleep; it's the perfect sleepy sandwich.

Bedtime -90 min.

DRINK CHERRY JUICE
Cherries are a natural source of the sleep hormone melatonin. Cherry juice drinkers fall asleep quicker and for longer.

Bedtime -1 hr

TAKE A HALF HOUR HOT BATH
Your body temperature drops when you sleep. You can prompt this sleepy state by stepping out of a hot bath.

Bedtime -45 min.

Say Goodnight to Your Phone

 Don't have your phone in your bedroom ...

 If you have your phone in your room, don't read it in bed ...

 If you read it in bed, turn down the backlight ...

 If you turn down the backlight, set yourself a time limit ...

 If you set a time limit, don't get on to social media ...

 If you get on to social media, don't read stressful stuff ...

 If you read stressful stuff, don't reply to it.

How to Wake Up in the Morning

1 You Snooze You Lose
Hitting the snooze button may leave you feeling more groggy and less refreshed.

2 Here Comes the Sun
Open your curtains as getting natural light in your room will wake you up.

3 Talk the Talk
Ask yourself good questions; what is it you want to achieve today?

4 Rise and Dine
Eating a good breakfast will improve your mood, memory and concentration during the day.

5 On Your Bike
Any early morning exercise will get your heart rate up, your blood flowing and improve your mood.

THE PERFECT WAY TO WAKE UP

Did you know that how you wake up is also really important? When you wake up your body goes through certain changes to help you feel fresh for the upcoming day: your body temperature increases, your sleep becomes lighter and particular hormones are released. But if you do certain things, this cycle can be affected and as a result your energy, alertness and concentration in the morning can suffer.

So what can you do to ensure you start the day well?

You snooze you lose

By pressing the snooze button you disrupt your natural sleep pattern, and instead of preparing your body to wake up your body may start preparing itself to go back to sleep. This means that when your alarm goes off again you wake up feeling groggier and less refreshed. This feeling can last for more than two hours after waking up.[94]

Here comes the sun

Do not get ready in the dark. Your body's internal clock (circadian rhythm) is linked to light and darkness. This has evolutionary roots: we hunted in the day and rested or hid from predators at night. This routine helped set our body clocks. We learnt to wake up when it was light because this was when we could best maximise our environment and surroundings.

As well as regulating your body clock, sunlight also affects levels of the hormone serotonin which is associated with well-being.[95] The more light you enjoy, the better you will feel. Open your curtains and let in the sun, or at least turn on the lights.

Ask yourself good questions

How you talk to yourself has a big impact on how you feel and perform. One early morning strategy you can use is to ask yourself questions such as, "What do I want to achieve today?" As well as helping you to manage any nerves or self-doubt, asking yourself this can also be motivating. One possible reason why this strategy is effective is because by asking yourself questions, your brain will automatically start searching for answers, acting as a call to action. So take heed of your inner narrative and start using it to your advantage.

Rise and dine

The ten minutes it takes to eat breakfast will benefit you more than an extra ten minutes in bed. If you are running late, the temptation may be to use snacks or energy drinks as a replacement for traditional breakfasts. However, eating cereal has been shown to help people improve their concentration and memory over the course of a morning.[96] This effect is not felt with energy drinks. This is because cereals that are rich in complex carbohydrates provide energy over the course of a whole morning, as opposed to energy drinks which may offer a short burst but are followed by a large slump.

Get moving

Exercise has many known benefits, both physically and psychologically. These include the fight against cancer, diabetes and heart disease, as well as improving our mood, energy levels and ability to cope with stressful situations. Exercising in the morning is good, as it is easy to put off being physically active when you are tired at the end of the day. An early morning workout can get your heart rate up and your blood flowing. You don't need to do a full gym session. If you go walking and can still talk but can't sing the words to your favourite song, then that is intense enough.

7 Reasons That Breakfast is Important

Enhances Memory
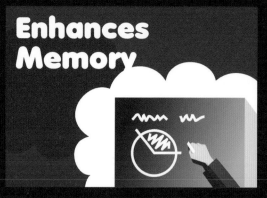

Increases Concentration

Improves Physical Health

Better Eating Habits That Day

Gives You Energy

Better Mental Health

Encourages Physical Activity

CHAPTER 8

LOOKING AFTER ME

HOW TO BE KIND TO YOURSELF

THE SCIENCE OF HAPPINESS

Did you know that, in the long term, Lottery winners tend not to be happier than anyone else?[97] This is because once the initial buzz of winning fades, people revert back to their normal happiness levels. So, if hitting the jackpot doesn't put a long lasting smile on your face, what does?

The Science of Happiness

- Don't make being happy your goal
- Connect with other people
- Prioritise time over money
- Do something kind for someone else
- Prioritise experiences over material things
- Exercise a little bit
- Embrace bad moods
- Remember your happiest moments in the past
- Spend some time outside
- Focus on what you have to look forward to in the future

Don't make being happy your goal

The more people strive to be happy, the less happy they are.[98] This is because instead of enjoying what they are doing, they are worrying whether they could be happier whilst doing it. They then feel disappointed when they don't reach this unobtainable happiness level. Being happy appears to be linked to embracing the present and not obsessing about the future or trying to be perfect.

Connect with other people

Spending time with other people and forming meaningful relationships makes people happier.[99] This seems to be especially true for students, who in a study reported feeling at their happiest when they were interacting with their friends, whilst being isolated corresponded to feeling at their saddest.[100]

Prioritise time over money

Evidence suggests that people who prioritise time over money report being happier.[101] This is probably because once time has gone, you can never get it back. That is not to say that money makes no impact. A study at Princeton University found that once people are paid US$75,000 a year (about £60,000), they don't report any increases in happiness.[102] Not having enough money can be a cause of stress and sadness, but having more than you need will not make you happier.

Do something kind for someone else

Doing something kind for someone else makes you feel happier.[103] Acts of kindness towards others increases happiness as it provides some novelty, reminds you that you are a good influence in the world and helps to foster positive relationships.

Prioritise experiences over material things

The problem with prioritising material things is that things change quickly.[104] Yesterday's desirable becomes today's essential, which in turn becomes tomorrow's relic. What was once seen as a bonus can quickly morph into a necessity. By prioritising experiences instead, you create life-long memories and develop more as a person.[105]

5 Ways to Manage Perfectionism

1. Become aware of perfectionism
2. Strive for excellence, not perfection
3. Develop a growth orientated mindset
4. Remember, nobody is perfect
5. Focus on enjoying and embracing the challenge

WAYS TO MANAGE PERFECTIONISM

People often feel under pressure to be perfect: perfectly smart, perfect looks, perfect at sport, perfect at socialising. Perfection is a myth. Trying to achieve it can quickly result in bitter disappointment and stress. Perfectionism is striving to achieve unobtainable goals and measuring yourself based only on your achievements.

If you set unobtainable goals and measure your self-worth against those goals, you are likely to be disappointed and angry when you inevitably fail. As singer Beyoncé remarked, "If everything was perfect, you would never learn and you would never grow." So how can we manage perfectionism?

Understand the cost of perfectionism

Being aware of the dangers of perfectionism can help start to protect you against them.[106] As well as hurting your general well-being, perfectionism can lead to a fear of failure. If your self-worth and identity are tied to your success, then you will tend to see mistakes and setbacks as a threat. The common perfectionist answer to this problem? Avoid situations that have an element of risk. Better to have the perception of perfect, rather than to risk it and let everyone see your imperfections. But, in reality, stepping out of your comfort zone gives you the space to learn and grow.

Strive for excellence, not perfection

Perfectionism is an illusion. Stop chasing this leprechaun and instead aim for high standards. By focusing on having an ethic of excellence, instead of chasing unobtainable perfectionism, you will enhance your resilience and reduce stress and anxiety, as well as improve your well-being.[107]

What is the difference between a culture of excellence and perfectionism? The former is focused on becoming as good as you can be and developing your skills. The latter focuses on not making any mistakes and avoiding looking bad. In a culture of excellence, mistakes are viewed as possible learning opportunities and not something to be covered up, embarrassed by or judged on. All you can do is work hard and be nice. Do the best you can. If you do that, you may not be perfect, but you will go to bed each night knowing you gave the best of yourself.

Develop a growth mindset

Developing a growth mindset is helpful as it shifts you towards improving your abilities and away from proving your abilities to others. This is an important distinction to understand. Instead of focusing on how smart you are, focus more on your attitude, effort and determination. This will help you to see yourself as a constant work in progress and so will motivate you to get better.

Remember, nobody is perfect

As we saw in Chapter 2, a lot of people today suffer from FOMO (Fear of Missing Out). Sometimes we see others living the 'perfect life' and try to measure up to that ideal. It can be a constant battle to remember that no one is as happy as they appear on Facebook or as wise as they appear on Twitter. By seeing what is going on 'behind the curtain', as well as developing skills such as self-compassion, we can all start to have a healthy relationship with our own flaws and understand that they are part of what makes us unique.

Focus on enjoying and embracing the challenge

The destination may not always be exactly what you thought it would be and doesn't last for very long – often the exciting bit is the journey itself. It would be a shame if you only embraced the 1% of the time that you are achieving your goal and not the 99% of the time it took to get there.

5 Ways to Improve Mental Well-being

1. CONNECT WITH OTHERS
2. GET ACTIVE
3. BE MINDFUL
4. KEEP LEARNING
5. GIVE TO OTHERS

HOW TO IMPROVE MENTAL HEALTH

When it comes to mental health, some people don't know where to begin or how to improve theirs. Fortunately, scientists have been examining the best ways to boost your mental health. It turns out that connecting with others, learning, giving, being physically active and improving our self-awareness is a good start.[108]

Connect with others

Having a range of healthy relationships matters. It is estimated that feeling disconnected from others is as bad for you as smoking 15 cigarettes a day. People who are more socially connected to family, friends and their communities are happier, physically healthier and live longer, with fewer mental health problems.[109] As well as forming connections on an individual level, being part of a group has similar benefits, as people who feel part of a group report being happier.[110]

Get active

As well as the physical benefits, exercise can also help to improve your mood, self-esteem and ability to deal with stress. The World Health Organization suggests that we should, on average, do about 22 minutes of moderate physical activity per day.[111] It's easy to be put off exercising if you feel tired or lazy. However, physical activity actually energises you. It refreshes and recharges you.

Be mindful

We live in an age of distraction. People check their phones on average 85 times a day.[112] This limits how much we notice what is going on around us. In 2007 the famous violinist Joshua Bell busked in disguise at a train station during rush hour in Washington; of the 1,097 people who passed him, only seven stopped to listen.[113] Only a few days before, people had paid hundreds of pounds to hear him play the same music, but as a busker very few would even give him the time of day. Would you have been one of those seven who stopped and listened?

Keep learning

Why does learning increase your mental well-being? As well as giving a sense of achievement, being enjoyable and helping you cope with stressful events, the feeling of learning, improving and getting better is a strong way to develop self-confidence.[114] Learning does not have to mean formal education. It can be as simple as reading a book. As Dr Seuss says, "The more that you read, the more things you will know. The more that you learn, the more places you'll go."

Give to others

Most people have heard the phrase, "It is better to give than receive." Economics research suggests that we feel a "warm glow" when we help someone else.[115] The power of giving is supported by research which found that random acts of kindness result in the giver feeling the benefit as well as the receiver.[116] So don't wait – go and do something nice for someone. You will feel better for it.

Challenging
Unhelpful Beliefs

 Look for proof that
the belief is true.

 Is there any evidence that
could change your mind?

 Examine the logic
of your belief.

 Are you thinking in extremes?
(i.e. 'always', 'must', 'every time')

 Question whether that
belief is helpful or not.

Based on research by @DrMJTurner and @DrJamieBarker

CHALLENGING UNHELPFUL BELIEFS

We've all had them: irrational thoughts that pop into our head without a moment's notice. And just like that, they can take hold. Fleeting moments of frustration become flat out anger. A passing worry takes grip and changes into anxiety and doubt. But what can you do about it?

This step-by-step guide provides a framework to help you challenge your unhelpful beliefs.[117]

Look for proof that the belief is true

A statement without proof is at best an opinion, and opinions can be wrong. As humans, we have a history of giving inaccurate opinions. For example, hardly anyone predicted the financial crash of 2008, many pundits tipped Leicester City to be relegated from the UK Premiership in 2016 before they went on to win the title,[118] and in 2006 Microsoft predicted that Apple wouldn't gain a sizeable share in the mobile phone sector.[119]

Before listening too much to that doubting voice in your head, first check for evidence. Is there any weight and credibility to justify it? If there is no proof, the thought is a speculative guess. React accordingly.

Is there any evidence that could change your mind?

This is a great question to ask yourself. It forces you to question whether you are blindly following false beliefs. If the answer to this question is no, then it means you could well be rejecting contrary evidence without properly considering it first.

Examine the logic of your belief

This is the culmination of the first two points. There are many reasons why your beliefs may not be logical. These include the confirmation bias (only agreeing with evidence that backs up your original belief), the bandwagon effect (believing something because everyone else does) and the negativity bias (paying more attention to negative information). Critically, calmly and rationally examine your beliefs in order to overcome these biases.

Are you thinking in extremes?

Things aren't always black or white. Life is more nuanced and messy than that. There are many shades of grey. If you are starting a sentence with words like 'Always' and 'Every time' or the phrase 'I must do this', then it is likely that you are missing some of the subtleties of the situation. The use of these superlatives could be an indication that your thoughts and beliefs are not as helpful to you as they could be.

Question whether that belief is helpful or not

This is not about seeing if your beliefs are positive or negative. It is more about working out if they are helpful or unhelpful. If you have followed the steps above and realised that some of your thoughts are unhelpful, it may be time to think differently.

WAYS to Get Out of a Bad Mood

1 Go For a Run
Exercise can improve mood as it releases hormones that can trigger positive feelings.

2 Be Optimistic
Expecting good things in the future can make you feel better.

3 Positive Imagery
Imagine your best possible self in the future. Once you know what you want, start working to achieve it.

4 Take a Deep Breath
This can help you to relax, take stock of the situation and think more clearly.

5 Take a Nap
Even a short nap can help you get out of a bad mood and perk you up.

6 Treat Yourself
'Retail therapy' has actually been found to improve mood. Buying yourself a small treat can make you feel better.

7 Listen to Music
Music has the power to enhance mood and improve how you are feeling.

CHAPTER 9

LESSONS FROM THE SPORTING GREATS

LEARN FROM CHAMPIONS

The Olympics:
What Separates
the Best From the Rest

They Do This	They Don't Do This
Are thoroughly prepared	Depart from normal routines
Arrive in peak physical condition	Over-train before the Games
Focus on what they can control	Get distracted by the media
Feel connected and trust their coach	Have ongoing issues with their coach
Feel connected to their team	Feel isolated or don't access support
Are committed to excellence	Get caught up in team politics
Embrace the realities of the Games	Get overawed by the scale of the Games

THE 1% MINDSET

Elite sportsmen and women are operating at the very top of their game.[120] They are examined on their skills, fitness, resilience and mindset on a frequent basis. Even if you don't like sport, there is a lot to learn from how athletes think. You can apply these lessons in your daily life in the quest to release your inner drive.

In sport the difference between success and failure is tiny. In the Olympics the difference in performance between gold and silver is typically less than 1%.[121] Often small differences add up to make a big difference.

One thing that sporting champions know is that these small differences are everywhere. It may be in what you eat, how you sleep, the way you learn and, above all, in the way you think. That is really what this book is about – exploring your true potential so you can get good at stuff. This chapter looks at what we can learn from these sporting greats.

The Psychology of Olympic Champions

100% Robust Confidence

Coachable and Open to Learning

Able to Manage Nerves

Resilient

 Sport Intelligence

 Able to Block Out Distractions

 Set Challenging and Realistic Goals

 Hopeful and Optimistic

 High Standards and Work Ethic

THE PSYCHOLOGY OF OLYMPIC CHAMPIONS

The Olympic motto 'Citius, Altius, Fortius', means 'Faster, Higher, Stronger'. It is easy to assume that this relates to athletes' physical abilities, but it is actually something much more than that. Citius, Altius, Fortius describes the mindset and mentality of our Olympians. It is a mindset we could all learn something from. So what makes up the mindset of an Olympic champion?[122]

Coachable and open to learning

Believing that you can get better and improve makes people seek out feedback, persist for longer and cope better with change. This is exciting because our mindsets can change and develop. A good starting point is to focus less on your natural ability and more on working with 100% effort and commitment.

Manage nerves and robust confidence

Delivering your best when it matters the most requires you to manage your nerves. It often takes athletes years of experience to work out how best to do this for themselves. This is one possible reason why many athletes don't medal in their first Olympic Games. So practise these skills as it takes patience and time to perfect them.

Challenging and realistic goals

In Chapter 1 we described the importance of owning the destination by setting challenging and realistic goals. Suffice to say, Olympic champions do goal setting very well. Their goals push them hard enough to keep them motivated, but are also realistic relative to their ability level so that they keep their enthusiasm high.

High standards and work ethic

There is an old saying that "Hard work beats talent when talent doesn't work hard." This is true in all walks of life – not just at the Olympics. Working hard doesn't guarantee success, but not working hard almost certainly guarantees failure.

Hopeful and optimistic

Being hopeful encapsulates the belief that tomorrow will be better than today. Having a sense of hope and optimism is a key component of developing grit and resilience.[123] Optimism refers to how you explain events that have happened. If you view setbacks as temporary then, rather than just giving up, you are more likely to work out how to overcome them.

Game intelligence and blocking out distractions

Game intelligence is a hard thing to quantify but it is a very valuable skill. It is about making good decisions very quickly based on what is happening whilst you compete. Being able to block out distractions helps athletes to do this. This is a hard ask at the Olympic Games, when athletes are all too aware of the consequences of their performance. But that just makes this skill even more valuable and decisive.

Resilience

We cover resilience in more detail later in this chapter as it is an important component of being a champion. But if you simply can't wait until then, we'll leave you with one tip on how to develop resilience: try viewing the decisions you make as active choices and not as sacrifices. By seeing them as a sacrifice, you will constantly be thinking about what you have given up and not about what you are working towards.

IF YOU CAN KEEP YOUR HEAD ...

If there is one passage of verse that sums up the psychology of Olympic champions, it is surely Rudyard Kipling's poem, 'If'.[124]

If

If you can keep your head when all about you
Are losing theirs and blaming it on you,
If you can trust yourself when all men doubt you,
But make allowance for their doubting too;
If you can wait and not be tired by waiting,
Or being lied about, don't deal in lies.
Or being hated, don't give way to hating,
And yet don't look too good, nor talk too wise:

If you can dream and not make dreams your master;
If you can think – and not make thoughts your aim;
If you can meet with Triumph and Disaster
And treat those two impostors just the same;
If you can bear to hear the truth you've spoken
Twisted by knaves to make a trap for fools,
Or watch the things you gave your life to, broken,
And stoop and build 'em up with worn-out tools:

If you can make one heap of all your winnings
And risk it on one turn of pitch-and-toss,
And lose, and start again at your beginnings
And never breathe a word about your loss;
If you can force your heart and nerve and sinew
To serve your turn long after they are gone
And so hold on when there is nothing in you
Except the Will which says to them: "Hold on!"

If you can talk with crowds and keep your virtue,
Or walk with Kings – nor lose the common touch,
If neither foes nor loving friends can hurt you,
If all men count with you, but none too much;
If you can fill the unforgiving minute
With sixty seconds' worth of distance run,
Yours is the Earth and everything that's in it,
And – which is more – you'll be a Man, my son!

HOW OLYMPIC CHAMPIONS DEVELOP RESILIENCE

Resilience is the ability to use your personal qualities to withstand pressure.[125] Being resilient helps you to overcome setbacks, and it drives you forward to bigger and better things than you had ever imagined. There has been a whole bunch of research into how Olympic champions develop their resilience.[126] So what can you learn from what they do?

9 Ways Olympic Champions Develop Resilience

1 Develop a positive personality

2 View decisions as active choices not sacrifices

3 Use support available from other people

4 Identify motivation for succeeding

5 Focus on personal development

6 View setbacks as an opportunity for growth

7 Strengthen confidence from a range of sources

8 Take responsibility for own thoughts, feelings and behaviours

9 Concentrate on what you can control

Develop a positive personality

Many Olympic champions talk about the importance of developing a 'positive personality'. This does not mean always and blindly believing you will win. Instead, it is about being open to new experiences and being optimistic, competitive and conscientious. It also includes being proactive. This means going out there and making it happen rather than waiting for things to happen.

View decisions as active choices not sacrifices

To the outside world it appears that becoming an Olympic champion requires a lot of sacrifice. But many Olympians don't see it as a sacrifice. Instead, they view it as an active choice. By viewing their commitment as an active choice and not as a sacrifice, they focus more on keeping their motivation levels high and less on what they are missing out on.

Use support available from other people

Seek out people who can help you. This can include technical advice on what you are doing or just social support to make you feel better when times are tough. As 17th century poet John Donne once said, "No man is an island". The more we isolate ourselves, the more we brood over bad decisions which increases our stress and frustration. As BT's slogan suggests, "It's good to talk".

Identify motivation for succeeding

Identifying what is important to you will help you to develop your drive forward. This will help to keep you motivated and determined, especially when you have had a setback or your goal seems far away.

Focus on personal development

Don't spend too much time comparing yourself to others. This can increase stress and the fear of failure. The race of life is long and, ultimately, you only compete with yourself.

View setbacks as an opportunity for growth

This is a key part of developing a growth mindset. You can do this yourself by asking what you have learnt from the experience and what you would do differently next time. In the long run setbacks can be beneficial and can help to spur you on.

Strengthen confidence from a range of sources

Drawing on a range of sources can make your self-confidence more robust.[127] This can include your preparation, your previous successes or the faith that other people have in your ability.

Take responsibility for own thoughts, feelings and behaviours

Ultimately, you are responsible for your thoughts, feelings and behaviours. No one else is. It is important to avoid the temptation of playing the blame game. Externalising your problems may protect your self-image for a little while, but it is unlikely to help you get better in the long run.[128]

Concentrate on what you can control

Focus on what you can control, not on what you can't change or can only influence. For Olympic champions, this means going out there and executing their game plan and their strategy as best as they can. That is all they have control over. If you do that well, you are more likely to secure the outcome you want.

5 Ways to Manage Your Nerves

1. **Reframing** – See things as an opportunity not a threat.

2. **Self-talk** – Talk to yourself in a positive, helpful and energised way.

3. **Picture perfect** – Visualise yourself performing successfully.

4. **Face your fears head on** – Focus on what you can do to make the situation better.

5. **Know that everyone gets nervous** – Nerves are normal and can help you do better.

HOW ATHLETES MANAGE NERVES

A student taking an exam shares similarities with an athlete competing on match day. Both require the ability to perform under pressure. Both require turning months, if not years, of hard work into a one-off performance.

You can use the same techniques that athletes use to manage your nerves. The context and situation may be different, but the strategies implemented to manage your emotions are the same. Here are some techniques that you can use to help keep your nerves in check.

Reframing

How do you see an upcoming event – as a challenge or a threat? You are more likely to view an event as a threat if you (a) focus on what it is you stand to lose, (b) feel the situation demands too much from you or (c) worry about looking bad. On the flipside, if you focus on what it is you stand to gain, feel you have the resources and skills necessary to meet the task and focus on mastery, then you are more likely to view the event as an opportunity.

Self-talk

How you talk to yourself can have a huge impact on how you think, feel and perform. For example, asking yourself questions ("Will I do well?") instead of making statements ("I will do well") helps to improve creativity as it puts you under less pressure.[129] Asking yourself questions is an effective technique when adopting new behaviours or when in unfamiliar situations.[130]

As well as asking yourself questions, telling yourself what to do can help you to improve attention and perform better under pressure.[131] This technique improves your self-control and ability to plan and prepare effectively.[132] Questions you should ask yourself are: "What do I need to do now?", "What has worked well in the past?" and "Am I on the right track?"

Picture perfect

As we saw in Chapter 4, picturing yourself performing an upcoming task really well increases your self-confidence.[133] Be careful, though, as too much time spent visualising can quickly translate into procrastination. However, if you have already done the hard work, spending a few minutes picturing it going well will ensure that you get all the psychological benefits, without the negative consequences of daydreaming the day away.

Face your fears head on

Facing your fears can help you to get better at the task at hand. Often things aren't as bad as we worry they will be. Once we face them head on we realise they are less daunting than we had imagined. Getting better at something is one of the most effective ways of improving your confidence and will help to reduce your nerves.

Remember that everyone gets nervous

The 'spotlight effect' describes how people tend to overestimate how much attention other people are paying to them. You feel like all eyes are on you, that you are the only one feeling nervous, that everyone is always calm and confident and they are judging you for being nervous. This could not be further from the truth. Every athlete gets nervous at some stage. Every student has moments of self-doubt. Remind yourself that these feelings are normal. As the old maxim says, "You wouldn't worry so much about what others think of you if you realised how seldom they do."

CHAPTER 10

MINDSET
MATTERS

STORIES AND SCIENCE
OF GROWTH MINDSET

Growth Mindset
Stories and Science

Overcome Setbacks

Larry Page co-founded Google but initially
he struggled to convince others of its value.
How did he cope with early setbacks? By
"having a healthy disregard for the impossible".

Masters Call it Practice

Thierry Henry scored 228 goals for Arsenal and is regarded
as one of their best ever players. But he didn't score for his first
eight games. His Twitter bio gives an insight into his mindset:
"Amateurs call it genius. Masters call it practice."

Raise Your Expectations

In round one of a study, people were asked to cycle 4,000m as fast as
they could. In round two, the same cyclists managed a much faster
time. Why? In round two, the cyclists thought they had raced against
their first ride, but really they had raced against a faster competitor.

Success Takes Time

Research has shown that it takes, on average, about 750 competitive
chess matches for a pro player to reach their peak in chess rankings.
There are no quick fixes. It takes many years of practice to get as
good as you can be.

Growth Mindset
Stories and Science

Overcome Setbacks

Just a few years before selling WhatsApp to Facebook for US$19 billion, Brian Acton was rejected by them at a job interview. He wrote, "Facebook turned me down. It was a great opportunity to connect with some fantastic people. Looking forward to life's next adventure."

Learn From Mistakes

Michael Jordan is the best basketball player ever. He offers an interesting insight into his mindset, when in a Nike advert he says that "I have failed over and over and over again in my life. And that is why I succeed."

Embrace the Challenge

Faced with a difficult task, what do you do? Research suggests that those with a growth mindset enjoy the challenge more and also want to persist with the task for longer.

Focus on Your Development

Studies have shown that those who focus on their own development, instead of comparing themselves to others, have higher levels of motivation, confidence, self-regulation and academic performance and less anxiety.

Growth Mindset
Stories and Science

Encourage Persistence

Olympic and world champion Jessica Ennis-Hill is a lot smaller than most of her rivals. Her coach, Toni Minichiello, helped her overcome this by helping her "not to give up and keep improving".

Better Than Yesterday

The first Harry Potter book, *Harry Potter and the Philosopher's Stone*, was rejected by 12 publishers. It was eventually accepted and went on to sell 107 million copies. J. K. Rowling's advice to students? "Just shoot for 'writing better than yesterday'."

Growth Mindset and Sense of Purpose

A recent study showed that combining growth mindset and sense of purpose interventions (highlighting how doing well at school can help achievement of their future goals) helps students improve their grades. This could be especially useful for students at risk of dropping out of school.

Feedback

In one of Carol Dweck's most famous studies, students were either praised for effort or ability. Those who had been praised for ability were more likely to ask for feedback on how they did at a task compared to others. Those who had been praised for effort wanted feedback on how they could get better.

Growth Mindset
Stories and Science

Champion Mindset

Muhammad Ali, arguably the greatest ever boxer, knew how important it was to work hard in training. He famously said, "I hated every minute of training, but I said, 'Don't quit. Suffer now and live the rest of your life like a champion!'"

Avoid Aiming for Perfection

Beyoncé has sold over 170 million records worldwide and won 20 Grammy awards. However, she advises against aiming for perfection, as "If everything was perfect, you would never learn and you would never grow."

Your Brain Can Grow

Research has shown that the more you engage in a task, the more parts of your brain develop. When taxi drivers studying for 'The Knowledge' were scanned, their hippocampus, the part of the brain associated with spatial awareness and memory, was shown to have grown significantly.

Transition and Resilience

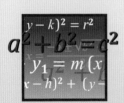

A study by David Yeager and Carol Dweck found that students with a growth mindset tend to cope better with transition in school. They also found that these students are more likely to finish challenging maths courses.

Growth Mindset
Stories and Science

Learning and Practising

When musician Ed Sheeran was asked about how he achieved his success, he replied, "When people say you are so talented and you're born with natural talent, I say 'no'. You have to really learn and really practice."

The Hungry Wolf

After winning his 11th Grand Slam, Novak Djokovic said "the wolf running up the hill [is] much hungrier than the wolf standing on the top of the hill … [the] mindset that one needs to have if one wants to stay up there … I think you need to work double as hard when you're up there."

Your Brain Can Develop

In a study of young children, researchers found that after one year of violin lessons, the part of their brain associated with music significantly developed. This shows that the brain is constantly changing and developing. It is not a fixed thing!

Higher Grades,
Better Mental Health

Research suggests that students who believe that intelligence can be developed achieve higher grades. Likewise, students who believe that they can learn to control their emotions report better mental health and fewer depressive symptoms.

Growth Mindset
Stories and Science

Focus on Developing Skills

Actor Will Smith makes an interesting distinction between talent and skill: "Your talent is going to fail you if you're not skilled." He adds: "Talent you have naturally. Skill is only developed by hours and hours of beating on your craft."

A Champion Mindset

Legendary tennis player Billie Jean King won an incredible 39 grand slams. How did she achieve so much? She gives an interesting insight into her mindset when she said, "Champions keep playing until they get it right."

Focus on the Process

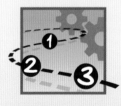

Recent research indicates that young children who had been praised by their parents for their processes (i.e. how they performed the task) and not just the outcome, were more likely to have a growth mindset five years on.

Better Responses to Setbacks

Studies show that when faced with a similar task to one that they have failed before, those praised for effort outperform their peers who have been praised for ability. This sort of praise also led to students enjoying the challenge more and they were less likely to lie about how well they had done.

WHAT NOW?

We hope you have enjoyed reading this book and looking at the illustrations. We like to help people change their lives for the better. But now it's up to you to do something. Hopes, dreams and good intentions mean nothing unless you take some action to make them happen. Go out there and start using some of the ideas, skills and strategies in this book. Answering the five questions on the next page will help you to do this.

If you want to, then go ahead and tear out the graphics in this book and stick them somewhere where they will remind you to action them. Or better still, go to our website www.innerdrive.co.uk and download them all for free. You can also follow us on Twitter @Inner_Drive.

Above all, get out there and do something that will make a difference. We are not saying it is going to be easy, but we are saying it is going to be worth it.

The 5 Best Questions To Ask

1

WHAT DO I NEED TO DO FIRST?
This question will help develop metacognition and get you started on the right path.

2

WHY IS THIS TRUE?
This is a great question to help improve memory and recall.

3

HOW can I GET BETTER?
Strengthen your growth mindset by focusing on how you can improve and develop.

4

WHO can I ASK FOR HELP?
Using the social support of people around you helps develop resilience.

5

WHERE DO I DO MY BEST WORK?
Improve your concentration by working somewhere with the fewest distractions.

SO YOU'VE READ THE BOOK AND LOVED IT.

What now?

1 | ADD US
Follow us on Twitter for more tips on how to get good at stuff @Inner_Drive.

2 | TAKE ACTION
Choose one area to master and start applying the strategies you've learnt. Goals without action are just dreams.

3 | SHARE YOUR GOAL
Tell a family member about the areas you are going to improve.

4 | TELL EVERYONE
Who else do you know who would benefit from getting this book?

5 | REVISIT IN ONE MONTH
It's amazing what you can pick up the second time you read a book.

6 | CHANGE SOMEONE'S LIFE
Leave this book somewhere someone else will pick it up and read it.

FOR TEACHERS AND PARENTS

We hope you enjoyed reading our book. More importantly, we hope your children or students take a lot from it and have started implementing some of the techniques we've discussed. If you want a copy of any of the graphics in the book, you can download them for free at www.innerdrive.co.uk by clicking on the 'Free Resources' link.

We know that knowledge learnt from research in psychology and neuroscience can help each and every student flourish and thrive. That's why we set up InnerDrive. We are fortunate to have worked with tens of thousands of students, teachers and parents in hundreds of schools across the UK, teaching them how to develop their mindsets and cultivate the key skills needed to perform under pressure.

Our school workshops help students, teachers and parents to release their inner drive. For more information about how we can help, please get in touch via info@innerdrive.co.uk and follow us on Twitter @Inner_Drive.

Thank you for your support.

ENDNOTES

Chapter 1

1   *The Oxford Book of English Verse 1250–1918*, ed. A. Quiller-Couch (Oxford: Oxford University Press, 1939).

2   E. A. Locke, Motivation through conscious goal setting. *Applied and Preventative Psychology*, 5(2) (1996), 117–124.

3   E. A. Locke and G. P. Latham, New directions in goal-setting theory. *Current Directions in Psychological Science*, 15(5) (2006), 265–268.

4   Locke, Motivation through conscious goal setting.

5   G. Oettingen, *Rethinking Positive Thinking: Inside the New Science of Motivation* (New York: Penguin, 2015).

6   B. Harkin, T. L. Webb, B. P. I. Chang, A. Prestwich, M. Conner, I. Kellar, Y. Benn and P. Sheeran, Does monitoring goal progress promote goal attainment? A meta-analysis of the experimental evidence. *Psychological Bulletin*, 142(2) (2016), 198–229.

Chapter 2

7   C. S. Dweck, *Mindset: How You Can Fulfil Your Potential* (New York: Ballantine, 2006).

8   J. Howard, *Getting Smart: The Social Construction of Intelligence* (Burlington, MA: Efficacy Institute, 1991).

9   D. M. Mueller and C. S. Dweck, Praise for intelligence can undermine children's motivation and performance. *Journal of Personality and Social Psychology*, 75(1) (1998), 33–52; L. S. Blackwell, K. H. Trzesniewski and C. S. Dweck, Implicit theories of intelligence predict achievement across an adolescent transition: a longitudinal study and an intervention. *Child Development*, 78(1) (2007), 246–263; D. Paunesku, G. M. Walton, C. Romero, E. N. Smith, D. S. Yeager and C. S. Dweck, Mind-set interventions are a scalable treatment for academic underachievement. *Psychological Science*, 26(6) (2015), 784–793; D. S. Yeager and C. S. Dweck, Mindsets that promote resilience: when students believe that personal characteristics can be developed. *Educational Psychologist*, 47 (2012), 302–314; J. Burnette, E. O'Boyle, E. Van Epps, J. Pollack and E. Finkel, Mind-sets matter: a meta-analytic review of implicit theories and self-regulation. *Psychological Bulletin*, 139(3) (2013), 655–670.

10   C. A. Wolters, S. L. Yu and P. R. Pintrich, The relation between goal orientation and students' motivational beliefs and self-regulated learning. *Learning and Individual Differences*, 8(3) (1996), 211–238.

11   See https://educationendowmentfoundation.org.uk/resources/teaching-learning-toolkit/meta-cognition-and-self-regulation/.

12   C. Hendrick and C. Hinton, Getting gritty with it: gritty students cultivate effective learning strategies and dispositions (working paper) (Cambridge, MA: Research Schools International, 2015).

13   W. Mischel, E. B. Ebbesen and Z. A. Raskoff, Cognitive and attentional mechanisms in delay of gratification. *Journal of Personality and Social Psychology*, 21(2) (1972), 204–218.

14   Y. Shoda, W. Mischel and P. K. Peake, Predicting adolescent cognitive and self-regulatory competencies from preschool delay of gratification: identifying diagnostic conditions. *Developmental Psychology*, 26(6) (1990), 978–986.

15   K. Fujita, On conceptualizing self-control as more than the effortful inhibition of impulses. *Personality and Social Psychology Review*, 15(4) (2011), 352–366.

16   A. Fishbach, R. S. Friedman and A. W. Kruglanski, Leading us not unto temptation: momentary allurements elicit overriding goal activation. *Journal of Personality and Social Psychology*, 84(2) (2003), 296–309.

17   A. Fishbach and J. Y. Shah, Self-control in action: implicit dispositions toward goals and away from temptations. *Journal of Personality and Social Psychology*, 90(5) (2006), 820–832.

18   P. Steel, The nature of procrastination: a meta-analytic and theoretical review of quintessential self-regulatory failure. *Psychological Bulletin*, 133(1) (2007), 65–94.

19   A. Klassen, L. Krawchuk and S. Rajani, Academic procrastination of undergraduates: low self-efficacy to self-regulate predicts higher levels of procrastination. *Contemporary Educational Psychology*, 33(4) (2008), 915–931.

20   R. Wiseman, *59 Seconds: Think a Little, Change a Lot* (London: Pan, 2010).

21   W. Eerde, A meta-analytically derived nomological network of procrastination. *Personality and Individual Differences*, 35(6) (2003), 1401–1418.

22   Steel, The nature of procrastination: a meta-analytic and theoretical review of quintessential self-regulatory failure.

23   P. Wright, J. Hollenbeck, S. Wolf and G. McMahan, The effects of varying goal difficulty operationalizations on goal setting outcomes and processes. *Organizational Behaviour and Human Decision Processes*, 66(1) (1995), 28–43.

24   J. C. Coulson, J. McKenna and M. Field, Exercising at work and self-reported work performance. *International Journal of Workplace Health Management*, 1(3) (2008), 176–197; K. Sellgren, Drinking water improves exam grades, research suggests. *BBC News* (18 April 2012). Available at: http://www.bbc.co.uk/news/education-17741653. See also: P. Booth, B. Taylor and C. J. Edmonds, Water supplementation improves visual attention and fine motor skills in schoolchildren. *Education and Health*, 30(3) (2012), 75–79; M. G. Berman, J. Jonides and S. Kaplan, The cognitive benefits of interacting with nature. *Psychological Science*, 19(12) (2008), 1207–1212; G. Felsten, Where to take a study break on the college campus: an attention restoration theory perspective. *Journal of Environmental Psychology*, 29(1) (2009), 160–167.

25   A. K. Przybylski, K. Murayama, C. R. DeHaan and V. Gladwell, Motivational, emotional, and behavioral correlates of fear of missing out. *Computers in Human Behavior*, 29(4) (2013), 1841–1848.

26   M. Khan, Adverse effects of excessive mobile phone use. *International Journal of Occupational Medicine and Environmental Health*, 21(4) (2008), 289–293.

27   Ofcom, A nation addicted to smartphones (4 August 2011). Available at: https://www.ofcom.org.uk/about-ofcom/latest/media/media-releases/2011/a-nation-addicted-to-smartphones.

Chapter 3

28   J. G. Nicholls, Achievement motivation: conceptions of ability, subjective experience, task choice, and performance. *Psychological Review*, 91(3) (1984), 328–346.

29 D. Lim and D. De Steno, Suffering and compassion: the links among adverse life experiences, empathy, compassion, and prosocial behavior. *Emotion*, 16(2) (2016), 175–182.

30 M. Sarkar, D. Fletcher and D. J. Brown, What doesn't kill me ...: adversity-related experiences are vital in the development of superior Olympic performance. *Journal of Science and Medicine in Sport*, 18(4) (2015), 475–479.

31 S. S. Sagar, B. K. Busch and S. Jowett, Success and failure, fear of failure, and coping responses of adolescent academy football players. *Journal of Applied Sport Psychology*, 22(2) (2010), 213–230.

32 J. G. Nicholls, Causal attributions and other achievement-related cognitions: effects of task outcome, attainment value, and sex. *Journal of Personality and Social Psychology*, 31(3) (1975), 379–389.

33 Wolters et al., The relation between goal orientation and students' motivational beliefs.

34 N. Silver, *The Signal and the Noise: The Art and Science of Prediction* (London: Penguin, 2013).

Chapter 4

35 M. J. Turner, M. V. Jones, D. Sheffield, J. Barker and P. Coffee, Manipulating cardiovascular indices of challenge and threat using resource appraisals. *International Journal of Psychophysiology*, 94(1) (2014), 9–18.

36 M. J. Turner, M. V. Jones, D. Sheffield and S. L. Cross, Cardiovascular indices of challenge and threat states predict competitive performance. *International Journal of Psychophysiology*, 86(1) (2012), 48–57.

37 M. J. Turner and J. B. Barker, Resilience: lessons from the 2012 Olympic Games. *Reflective Practice*, 14(5) (2013), 622–631.

38 A. Bandura, Self-efficacy: toward a unifying theory of behavioural change. *Psychological Review*, 84(2) (1977), 191–215.

39 R. C. Wilson, P. J. Sullivan, N. D. Myers and D. L. Feltz, Sources of sport confidence of master athletes. *Journal of Sport and Exercise Psychology*, 26(3) (2004), 369–384.

40 M. Machida, R. M. Ward and R. S. Vealey, Predictors of sources of self-confidence in collegiate athletes. *International Journal of Sport and Exercise Psychology*, 10(3) (2012), 172–185.

41 A. Miles and R. Neil, The use of self-talk during elite cricket batting performance. *Psychology of Sport and Exercise*, 14(6) (2013), 874–881.

42 A. Hatzigeorgiadis, Instructional and motivational self-talk: an investigation on perceived self-talk functions. *Hellenic Journal of Psychology*, 3(2) (2006), 164–175.

43 E. A. Holmes, A. Mathews, T. Dalgleish and B. Mackintosh, Positive interpretation training: effects of mental imagery versus verbal training on positive mood. *Behavior Therapy*, 37(3) (2006), 237–247.

44 G. Mamassis and G. Doganis, The effects of a mental training program on juniors pre-competitive anxiety, self-confidence, and tennis performance. *Journal of Applied Sport Psychology*, 16(2) (2002), 118–137.

45 G. M. Bakker, In defence of thought stopping. *Clinical Psychologist*, 13(2) (2009), 59–68.

46   G. Godin, A. Belanger-Gravel, L. A. Vezina-Im, S. Amireault and A. Bilodeau, Question-behaviour effect: a randomized controlled trial of asking intention in the interrogative or declarative form. *Psychological Health*, 27(9) (2012), 1086–1099.

47   E. Watson, Gender equality is your issue too. Speech at the launch of the HeForShe campaign, United Nations Headquarters, New York, 20 September 2014.

48   Miles and Neil, The use of self-talk.

49   D. H. Meichenbaum and J. Goodman, Training impulsive children to talk to themselves: a means of developing self-control. *Journal of Abnormal Psychology*, 77(2) (1971), 115–126.

50   Hatzigeorgiadis, Instructional and motivational self-talk.

51   P. C. Burnett, Children's self-talk and academic self-concepts: the impact of teachers' statements. *Educational Psychology in Practice*, 15(3) (1999), 195–200.

52   E. Kross, E. Bruehlman-Senecal, J. Park, A. Burson, A. Dougherty, H. Shablack, R. Bremner and J. Moser, Self-talk as a regulatory mechanism: how you do it matters. *Journal of Personality and Social Psychology*, 106(2) (2014), 304–324.

53   K. Theide, M. Anderson and D. Therriault, Accuracy of metacognitive monitoring affects learning of texts. *Journal of Educational Psychology*, 95(1) (2003), 66–73.

54   A. Bandura and E. A. Locke, Negative self-efficacy and goal effects revisited. *Journal of Applied Psychology*, 88(1) (2003), 87–99.

55   J. B. Vancouver, C. M. Thompson and A. A. Williams, The changing signs in the relationships among self-efficacy, personal goals, and performance. *Journal of Applied Psychology*, 86(4) (2001), 605–620.

56   S. L. Beilock, C. A. Kulp, L. E. Holt and T. H. Carr, More on the fragility of performance: choking under pressure in mathematical problem solving. *Journal of Experimental Psychology*, 133(4) (2004), 584–600.

Chapter 5

57   M. T. Timlin, M. A. Pereira, M. Story and D. Neumark-Sztainer, Breakfast eating and weight change in a 5-year-prospective analysis of adolescents: Project EAT (Eating Among Teens). *Pediatrics*, 121(3) (2008), 638–645.

58   K. A. Wesnes, C. Pincock, D. Richardson, G. Helm and S. Hails, Breakfast reduces declines in attention and memory over the morning in schoolchildren. *Appetite*, 41(3) (2003), 329–331.

59   Berman et al., The cognitive benefits of interacting with nature.

60   Coulson et al., Exercising at work and self-reported work performance.

61   J. Dunlosky, K. A. Rawson, E. J. Marsh, M. J. Nathan and D. T. Willingham, Improving students' learning with effective learning techniques: promising directions from cognitive and educational psychology. *Psychological Science in the Public Interest*, 14(1) (2013), 4–58.

62   N. Perham and H. Currie, Does listening to preferred music improve reading comprehension performance? *Applied Cognitive Psychology*, 28 (2014), 279–284.

63   D. Benton, Dehydration influences mood and cognition: a plausible hypothesis? *Nutrients*, 3(5) (2011), 555–573.

64   B. Thornton, A. Faires, M. Robbins and E. Rollins, The mere presence of a cell phone may be distracting: implications for attention and task performance. *Social Psychology*, 45(6) (2014), 479–488.

65   K. Anders Ericsson and R. Pool, *Peak: Secrets from the New Science of Expertise* (New York: Houghton Mifflin Harcourt, 2016).

66   G. Miller, The magical number seven, plus or minus two: some limits on our capacity for processing information. *Psychological Review*, 63(2) (1956), 81–97.

67   A. S. Benjamin and J. Tullis, What makes distributed practice effective? *Cognitive Psychology*, 61(3) (2010), 228–247.

68   P. A. Cohen, J. A. Kulik and C. C. Kulik, Educational outcomes of tutoring: a meta-analysis of findings. *American Educational Research Journal*, 19(2) (1982), 237–248.

69   S. K. Carpenter, Cue strength as a moderator of the testing effect: the benefits of elaborative retrieval. *Journal of Experimental Psychology: Learning, Memory, and Cognition*, 35 (2009), 1563–1569.

70   M. Pressley, M. A. McDaniel, J. E. Turnure, E. Wood and M. Ahmad, Generation and precision of elaboration: effects on intentional and incidental learning. *Journal of Experimental Psychology: Learning, Memory, and Cognition*, 13(2) (1987), 291–300.

71   O. Adesope, D. A. Trevisan and N. Sundararajan, Rethinking the use of tests: a meta-analysis of practice testing. *Review of Educational Research*, 20(10), 1–43.

72   J. Reeve, H. Jang, P. Hardre and M. Omura, Providing a rationale in an autonomy-supportive way as a strategy to motivate others during an uninteresting activity. *Motivation and Emotion*, 26(3) (2002), 183–207.

73   D. Carrington, Three-quarters of UK children spend less time outdoors than prison inmates – survey. *The Guardian* (25 March 2016).

74   C. Capaldi, R. L. Dopko and J. M. Zelenski, The relationship between nature connectedness and happiness: a meta-analysis. *Frontiers in Psychology*, 5 (2014), 976. DOI: 10.3389/fpsyg.2014.00976.

75   Berman et al., The cognitive benefits of interacting with nature.

76   A. P. Smith, Breakfast and mental health. *International Journal of Food Science Nutrition*, 49(5) (1998), 397–402.

Chapter 6

77   Dunlosky et al., Improving students' learning with effective learning techniques.

78   H. Rodiger and J. Karpicke, Test enhanced learning. *Association for Psychological Science*, 17(3) (2006), 249–255.

79   S. Cotterill, Pre-performance routines in sport: current understanding and future directions. *International Review for Sport and Exercise Psychology*, 3(2) (2010), 132–153; T. Murphy and T. Orlick, Mental strategies of professional actors. *Journal of Excellence*, 11 (2006), 103–125.

80   K. Desender, S. Beurms and E. V. den Bussche, Is mental effort exertion contagious? *Psychonomic Bulletin & Review*, 23 (2) (2016), 624–631.

81   B. Walsh, *The Score Takes Care of Itself: My Philosophy of Leadership* (New York: Penguin, 2010).

82   See http://www.nhs.uk/Conditions/stress-anxiety-depression/Pages/ways-relieve-stress.aspx.

83   See https://educationendowmentfoundation.org.uk/resources/teaching-learning-toolkit/meta-cognition-and-self-regulation/.

Chapter 7

84 K. M. Orzech, C. Acebo, R. Seifer, D. Barker and M. A. Carskadon, Sleep patterns are associated with common illness in adolescents. *Journal of Sleep Research*, 23(2) (2014), 133–142.

85 P. Alhola and P. Polo-Kantola, Sleep deprivation: impact on cognitive performance. *Neuropsychiatric Disease and Treatment*, 3(5) (2007), 553–567.

86 M. L. Wong, E. Y. Y. Lau, J. H. Y. Wan, S. F. Cheung, H. Hui and D. S. Y. Mok, The interplay between sleep and mood in predicting academic functioning, physical health and psychological health: a longitudinal study. *Journal of Psychosomatic Research*, 74(4) (2013), 271–277.

87 W. E. Kelly, K. E. Kelly and R. C. Clanton, The relationship between sleep-length and grade-point average among college students. *College Student Journal*, 35(1) (2001), 84–86.

88 National Sleep Foundation, *Teens and Sleep* (Washington, DC: National Sleep Foundation, 2006).

89 National Sleep Foundation, How much sleep do we really need? (2015). Available at: https://sleepfoundation.org/how-sleep-works/how-much-sleep-do-we-really-need.

90 Toure, Adele opens up about her inspirations, looks and stage fright. *Rolling Stone* (28 April 2011).

91 L. Foley, R. Maddison, Y. Jiang, S. Marsh, T. Olds and K. Ridley, Presleep activities and time of sleep onset in children. *Pediatrics*, 31(2) (2013), 276–282.

92 B. Wood, M. S. Rea, B. Plitnick and M. G. Figueiro, Light level and duration of exposure determine the impact of self-luminous tablets on melatonin suppression. *Applied Ergonomics*, 44(2) (2013), 237–240.

93 G. Howatson, P. Bell, J. Tallent, B. Middleton, M. McHugh and J. Ellis, Effect of tart cherry juice (*Prunus cerasus*) on melatonin levels and enhanced sleep quality. *European Journal of Nutrition*, 51(8) (2012), 909–916; S. L. Halson, Sleep in elite athletes and nutritional interventions to enhance sleep. *Sports Medicine*, 44(1) (2014), 13–23.

94 A. Brooks and L. Lack, A brief afternoon nap following nocturnal sleep restriction: which nap duration is most recuperative? *Sleep*, 29(6) (2006), 831–840.

95 G. Lambert, C. Reid, D. Kaye, G. Jennings and M. Esler, Effect of sunlight and season on serotonin turnover in the brain. *Lancet*, 260(9348) (2002), 1840–1842.

96 Wesnes et al., Breakfast reduces declines in attention and memory.

Chapter 8

97 P. Brickman, D. Coates and R. Janoff-Bulman, Lottery winners and accident victims: is happiness relative? *Journal of Personality and Social Psychology*, 36(8) (1978), 917–927.

98 I. B. Mauss, M. Tamir, C. L. Anderson and N. S. Savino, Can seeking happiness make people unhappy? Paradoxical effects of valuing happiness. *Emotion*, 11(4) (2011), 807–815.

99 D. Kahneman, A. B. Krueger, D. A. Schkade, N. Schwarz and A. A. Stone, A survey method for characterising daily life experience: the day reconstruction method. *Science*, 306(5702) (2004), 1776–1780.

100 M. Csikszentmihalyi and J. Hunter, Happiness in everyday life: the uses of experience sampling. *Journal of Happiness Studies*, 4(2) (2003), 185–199.

101 A. V. Whillans, A. C. Weidman and E. W. Dunn, Valuing time over money is associated with greater happiness. *Social Psychological and Personality Science*, 7(3) (2016), 213–222.

102 B. Luscombe, Do we need $75,000 a year to be happy? *Time* (6 September 2010).

103 S. Lyubomirsky, K. M. Sheldon and D. Schkade, Pursuing happiness: the architecture of sustainable change. *Review of General Psychology*, 9(2) (2005), 111–113.

104 P. Pchelin and R. T. Howell, The hidden cost of value-seeking: people do not accurately forecast the economic benefits of experiential purchases. *Journal of Positive Psychology*, 9(4) (2014), 322–334.

105 M. Yamaguchi, A. Masuchi, D. Nakanishi, S. Suga, N. Konishi, Y. Y. Yu and Y. Ohtsubo, Experiential purchases and prosocial spending promote happiness by enhancing social relationships. *Journal of Positive Psychology*, 11(5) (2016), 480–488.

106 M. A. Aldea, K. G. Rice, B. Gormley and A. Rojas, Telling perfectionists about their perfectionism: effects of providing feedback on emotional reactivity and psychological symptoms. *Behaviour Research and Therapy*, 48(12) (2010), 1194–1203.

107 G. L. Flett and P. L. Hewitt, A proposed framework for preventing perfectionism and promoting resilience and mental health among vulnerable children and adolescents. *Psychology in the Schools*, 51(9) (2014), 899–912.

108 See http://www.nhs.uk/Conditions/stress-anxiety-depression/Pages/improve-mental-wellbeing.aspx.

109 See https://www.mentalhealth.org.uk.

110 J. Wakefield, F. Sani, M. Vishnu, M. Norbury, P. Dugard, C. Gabbanelli, M. Arnetoli, G. Beconci, L. Botindari, F. Grifoni, P. Paoli and F. Poggesi, The relationship between group identification and satisfaction with life in a cross-cultural community sample. *Journal of Happiness Studies* (2016). DOI: 10.1007/s10902-016-9735-z.

111 See http://www.who.int/dietphysicalactivity/factsheet_adults/en/.

112 S. Andrews, D. Ellis, H. Shaw and L. Piwek, Beyond self-report: tools to compare estimated and real-world smartphone use. *PloS ONE*, 10(10) (2015): e0139004.

113 T. Service, Joshua Bell: no ordinary busker. *The Guardian* (18 April 2007).

114 T. Scjuller, A. Brassett-Grundy, A. Green, C. Hammond and J. Preston, *Learning, Continuity and Change in Adult Life*. Research Report no. 3 (London: Centre for Research on the Wider Benefits of Learning, 2002).

115 A. James, Impure altruism and donations to public goods: a theory of warm-glow giving. *Economic Journal*, 100(401) (1990), 464–477.

116 S. Lyubomirsky and K. Layous, How do simple positive activities increase well-being. *Current Directions in Psychological Science*, 22(1) (2013), 57–62.

117 Based on research by Dr Martin Turner and Dr Jamie Barker at the Smarter Thinking Project: http://thesmarterthinkingproject.com/.

118 Premier League 2015–16: Guardian football writers' season predictions, *The Guardian* (5 August 2015).

119 R. J. Szczerba, 15 worst tech predictions of all time. *Forbes* (5 January 2015).

Chapter 9

120 C. Greenleaf, D. Gould and K. Dieffenbach, Factors influencing Olympic performance: interviews with Atlanta and Nagano U.S. Olympians. *Journal of Applied Sport Psychology*, 13(2) (2001), 154–184.

121 Analysis of London 2012 Olympics results by InnerDrive.

122 D. Gould, K. Dieffenbach and A. Moffett, Psychological characteristics and their development in Olympic champions. *Journal of Applied Sport Psychology*, 14(3) (2002), 172–204.

123 A. Duckworth, *Grit: The Power of Passion and Perseverance* (New York: Scribner, 2016).

124 R. Kipling, *Rewards and Fairies* (Garden City, NY: Doubleday, Page & Co., 1910).

125 D. Fletcher and M. Sarkar, Mental fortitude training: an evidence-based approach to developing psychological resilience for sustained success. *Journal of Sport Psychology in Action*, 7(3) (2016), 135–157.

126 For example, D. Fletcher and M. Sarkar, A grounded theory of psychological resilience in Olympic champions. *Psychology of Sport and Exercise*, 13(5) (2012), 669–678.

127 M. Machida, R. M. Ward and R. S. Vealey, Predictors of sources of self-confidence in collegiate athletes. *International Journal of Sport and Exercise Psychology*, 10(3) (2012), 172–185.

128 Sagar et al., Success and failure.

129 I. Senay, D. Albarracin and K. Noguchi, Motivating goal-directed behavior through introspective self-talk: the role of the interrogative form of simple future tense. *Psychological Science*, 21(4) (2010), 499–504.

130 Godin et al., Question-behaviour effect.

131 Miles and Neil, The use of self-talk.

132 Meichenbaum and Goodman, Training impulsive children to talk to themselves.

133 Mamassis and Doganis, The effects of a mental training program.

Chapter 10

134 M. R. Stone, K. Thomas, M. Wilkinson, A. M. Jones, A. St Clair Gibson and K. G. Thompson, Effects of deception on exercise performance: implications for determinants of fatigue in humans. *Medicine & Science in Sports & Exercise*, 44(3) (2012), 534–541; R. W. Howard, Individual differences in expertise development over decades in a complex intellectual domain. *Memory & Cognition*, 37(2) (2009), 194–209.

135 C. M. Mueller and C. S. Dweck, Praise for intelligence can undermine children's motivation and performance. *Journal of Personality and Social Psychology*, 75(1) (1998), 33–52; Wolters et al., The relation between goal orientation and students' motivational beliefs.

136 Paunesku et al., Mind-set interventions are a scalable treatment; Mueller and Dweck, Praise for intelligence can undermine children's motivation.

137 E. A. Maguire, D. G. Gadian, I. S. Johnsrude, C. D. Good, J. Ashburner, R. S. J. Frackowiak and C. D. Frith, Navigation-related structural change in the hippocampi of taxi drivers. *Proceedings of the National Academy of Sciences of the United States of America*, 97(8) (2000), 4398–4403; Yeager and Dweck, Mindsets that promote resilience.

138 T. Fujioka, B. Ross, R. Kakigi, C. Pantev and L. J. Trainor, One year of musical training affects development of auditory cortical-evoked fields in young children. *Brain*, 129 (2006), 2593–2608; C. Romero, A. Master, D. Paunesku, C. S. Dweck and J. J. Gross, Academic and emotional functioning in middle school: the role of implicit theories. *Emotion*, 14(2) (2014), 227–234.

139 E. A. Gunderson, S. J. Gripshover, C. Romero, C. S. Dweck, S. Goldin-Meadow and S. C. Levine, Parent praise to 1- to 3-year-olds predicts children's motivational frameworks 5 years later. *Child Development*, 84(5) (2013), 1526–1541; Mueller and Dweck, Praise for intelligence can undermine children's motivation.

InnerDrive runs workshops and mentoring that can help people realise their potential.

We can help you improve your mindset, motivation, resilience and performance under pressure.

InnerDrive can offer:

Schools
Great workshops for students, staff and parents.

Athletes
Mentoring to help you consistently perform at a higher level.

Businesses
Workshops for teams and mentoring for leaders.

InnerDrive has successfully helped international footballers and team GB athletes, as well as over 200 schools, 50,000 students and many companies, improve their performance. Our workshops are of the highest quality. They are based on the latest research, teach strategies that can be applied to real life and are fun and interactive.

If you want high quality workshops or mentoring, contact us via our website (www.innerdrive.co.uk), by email (info@innerdrive. co.uk) or by phone (0208 693 3191).

InnerDrive

www.innerdrive.co.uk   @Inner_Drive